THE
FETHARD-ON-SEA
BOYCOTT

Tim Fanning grew up in Dublin. Since studying history in UCD, he has worked as a journalist in Ireland and Spain. He has written on Irish history and politics for the regional and national press. In the mid-1980s, as a young boy, he spent his summer holidays in Fethard-on-Sea where he first learnt about the boycott and got to know the Cloney family.

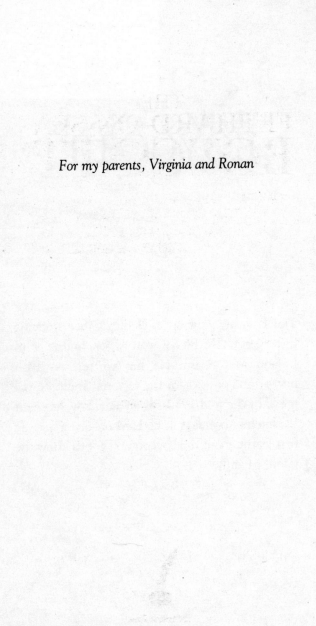

For my parents, Virginia and Ronan

THE
FETHARD-ON-SEA
BOYCOTT

IRELAND 1957...
  THE CATHOLIC CHURCH...
    A SMALL VILLAGE...
      A MIXED MARRIAGE...

Tim Fanning

The Collins Press

First published in 2010 by
The Collins Press
West Link Park
Doughcloyne
Wilton
Cork

Reprinted 2010

Photographs courtesy of the Cloney family unless otherwise credited.

Tim Fanning has asserted his moral right to be identified as the author of this work.

British Library Cataloguing in Publication Data

Fanning, Tim.
  The Fethard-on-Sea boycott.
  1. Cloney family. 2. Fethard-on-Sea (Ireland)—Social
  conditions—20th century. 3. Boycotts—Ireland—
  Fethard-on-Sea. 4. Communalism—Ireland—Fethard-on-Sea.
  5. Catholic Church—Education—Ireland—History—20th
  century. 6. Fortune, Sean, d. 1999. 7. Child sexual abuse
  by clergy—Ireland—Fethard-on-Sea.
  I. Title
  941.8'850823-dc22

ISBN-13: 9781848890329

Typesetting by The Collins Press
Typeset in Goudy and Gilgamesh Medium
Printed in Great Britain by J F Print Ltd

Cover photographs
Front and spine: Seán, Sheila, Eileen and Mary Cloney in the kitchen of Dungulph Castle in January 1958. *Back* (top, l–r)): Eileen Cloney, Seán and Sheila on their wedding day, Mary Cloney, Dungulph Castle; (bottom): Mary Cloney (far left) and Eileen Cloney (fifth from right) on Westray in the Orkney Islands during the boycott.

Contents

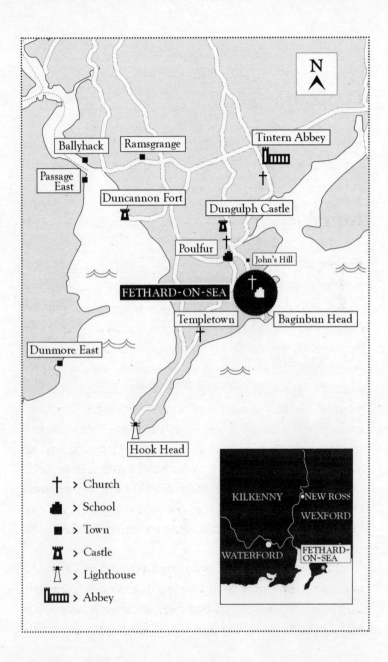

Introduction

The Hook Peninsula in County Wexford is one of the most attractive, if less well-known, parts of the country. It is not a rugged beauty like that of Connemara or Donegal. Nor is it that spectacular beauty to be found in Kerry or Clare. Instead, it has a remote, otherworldly mystery all of its own. There are few places where the past seems to hang so heavily in the air, from the haunted Victorian grandeur of Loftus Hall to the Cistercian splendour of Tintern Abbey. Fethard-on-Sea lies on the eastern side of the Hook at the entrance to Bannow Bay. Its quaint appendix, redolent of the somnolent English seaside, distinguishes the Wexford village from the landlocked town of Fethard in County Tipperary. Fethard is a quiet spot, only becoming busy during the summer months when the tourists arrive.

I first visited Fethard as an eight-year-old in 1984. My uncle and aunt, over from London, had rented Dungulph Castle, a Norman-era fortified dwelling about a mile and a half outside Fethard, and had invited my parents and me to join them and my cousins for a family holiday. The castle is an impressive building, especially for eight-year-olds with active imaginations. Built by the Whitty family in the fifteenth century, it still has many of its original defensive features, including a tower with arrow slits, a turret and a machicolation from which stones or burning hot pitch could be dropped on the enemy. It has a venerable history, withstanding siege and arson over the years. In 1642, a party of English soldiers from nearby Duncannon Fort attacked rebels who were holed up in the castle. The defenders managed to beat them back. The bodies of sixteen of the soldiers are believed to be buried in the vicinity. The Devereux family, one of the foremost rebel families on the Hook, were tenants during the 1798 Rebellion. The castle was burnt in reprisal. The Cloney family moved in shortly afterwards.

The castle was divided in two in the 1980s. One side was given over to paying guests. Seán and Sheila Cloney lived in the other side. The Cloneys were farmers. Being from Dublin and with little experience of the country, I was fascinated by the farm and thrilled to be allowed help bring the cows in for milking or gather the hay. In this way, I got to know the Cloney family – Seán and Sheila, their daughters, Eileen, Mary and Hazel, and their grandchildren. Seán and Sheila were then in their late fifties. Seán was a rather unusual character, not at all the archetype of the Irish farmer. He wore a beret, de rigueur perhaps for his brethren in Provence or the Basque country, but a rare enough sight in rural Ireland. He had a slight stoop owing to a problem with his spine, and piercing blue eyes which gave him an owlish demeanour that went hand in hand with his talent for storytelling and his love of learning. He was a great conversationalist, someone with a natural curiosity about other people. Sheila, on the other hand, was less visible. Whereas Seán was often to be found pottering about the farmyard, eager for a chat, Sheila was more shy and rarely emerged from the other side of the castle.

During that summer and on return visits to Fethard, Seán shared his considerable knowledge of the Hook with our family. He was a keen local historian, particularly interested in the Colclough family, who had lived in the nearby Tintern Abbey from the suppression of the monasteries in the sixteenth century right up until the middle of the twentieth century when the last resident handed the abbey over to the care of the State. Such was his enthusiasm for history that, after the day's work, he would retreat to his study on the top floor of the castle and spend hours poring over his research. Often he would work into the early hours of the morning. When correspondents from all over the world would get in touch with him looking for information about some distant forebear who lived on the Hook, he would respond graciously, even though it meant he had less time for his own researches.

One evening, as the sun was going down on a glorious summer's day, I was standing in the farmyard with Seán and my father. They were leaning on a gate in the farmyard, chatting. My father mentioned that we had made a pit stop earlier that day at Loftus Hall, the hulking Victorian mansion close to Hook Head. The Marquis of Ely, the principal landowner on the Hook, had built Loftus Hall on the site of a previous building towards the end of the nineteenth century. It was an unpropitious time to embark on such an ambitious project. Building work began in 1870, the year of Gladstone's first Land Act. During the next decade, the worsening economic situation on the land, caused by a slump in agricultural prices, led to increased agrarian agitation. The Land War, which was particularly violent on the Hook, eventually ended in defeat for the old ascendancy landlords. In 1913, the Ely estate put Loftus Hall up for sale. It became a Benedictine and, later, a Rosminian convent. In the early 1980s, it was privately owned and was run as a hotel. I had found the place intriguing. As my mother and father had a drink – we were the only customers in the deserted bar – I had wandered off on my own to explore the long, empty hallways. By the time we arrived back at Dungulph, I was well acquainted with its nooks and crannies.

After chatting with my father about the history of The Hall, as it was known locally, Seán turned to me and asked did I know that it was haunted. I said I did not. With a mischievous grin, he began telling me about a foul, stormy night many years before when a stranger on horseback knocked on the door of Loftus Hall – then owned by the Tottenham family – looking for shelter. After giving him something to eat and drink, the head of the family, Charles Tottenham, invited his guest to a game of cards. Also present was Tottenham's daughter, Anne, who immediately took a fancy to the handsome young stranger. However, during the game, when Anne dropped one of her cards and bent down to pick it up, she discovered that where the handsome stranger's foot should have been, there was instead a cloven hoof. She let out a most dreadful scream. Whereupon the Devil revealed himself and shot through the ceiling, leaving a crack which could never be repaired. Poor Anne went instantly mad and was locked in her room, never to emerge again. She was buried in one of the closets. Seán looked me in the eye. 'And her ghost still haunts Loftus Hall,' he said. A cold shiver ran through me as I recalled my wanderings alone around the deserted mansion earlier that day.

On the last night of our holiday, my uncle invited Seán to join us in the sitting room on 'our' side of the castle for a farewell drink. The room was full, the adults chatting among themselves, the children switching in and out of their conversation. Then, my father, also a historian, asked Seán did he know anything about the infamous boycott which had taken place in Fethard in the 1950s. A grin came across Seán's face; he paused and replied, 'I should. I was the man involved.' There was a moment's silence. The rest of us non-historians wondered why my father looked so sheepish.

That was the first time I had heard about the boycott. I was only eight years old and didn't think much more of it for many years – the story of Loftus Hall had a greater impact on me. My summers in Fethard were taken up with exploring the farm or being taught the rudiments of hurling by Seán's grandson David. But bit by bit, over the years, I learnt more about the story and became fascinated. Seán was a Catholic. His wife, Sheila, was a Protestant. They had initially agreed that their children would be raised in both traditions. But Sheila had signed a piece of paper promising to raise the children as Catholics when she got married, as was prescribed by Catholic teaching. Eight years later, when it was time for the Cloneys' eldest daughter, Eileen, to begin her schooling, Sheila decided that it was up to herself and

Seán to make the decision about which school she would attend. The local Catholic clergy disagreed and told her, in no uncertain terms, that Eileen was to be sent to the Catholic school. Refusing to be told what to do by the priests, Sheila left home with her two daughters, whereupon the Catholics of the village, at the bidding of the two local priests, began a boycott of the Protestant-owned shops and farms in Fethard.

Fifteen years later I returned to Fethard. Seán was no longer the sprightly man I remembered as a young boy. He was now paralysed from the neck down after a procedure to fix a halo brace following a road accident had gone horribly wrong in a Dublin hospital. His body was broken but his eyes retained their warmth and sense of humour. In my hand, I had a letter that I had found in the archives from a local man, John Joe Ryan, to the Taoiseach of the day, Éamon de Valera, which contained an intriguing line suggesting that the roots of the boycott went back eighty years. I quizzed Seán about the reference, and the conversation which followed led me to investigate the deep historical resentments and grievances which had surfaced during the boycott.

I discovered that the boycott resulted as much from economic motives as from sectarian ones. The local Catholic clergy were anxious to prevent a situation where substantial-sized Catholic-owned farms fell into the hands of children who might be reluctant to contribute to parochial revenues. Once the boycott began, some Catholic traders saw an opportunity to get rid of unwelcome competition in the form of Protestant shops. The remainder of the Catholics in the village, who had hitherto enjoyed friendly if somewhat

Introduction

distant relations with their Protestant neighbours, were bullied into acquiescing to the boycott out of simple fear.

Some writers and historians contend that the Protestant minority enjoyed remarkable toleration after Independence, and that the boycott was a blip. In fact, Fethard is a blip, but only because Sheila Cloney, unlike so many others among her co-religionists, stood up to the bullies. The Protestant minority were tolerated because they kept their heads down and, for the most part, accepted that the Catholic Church would have an uncommon amount of influence in matters more properly the business of the State or individual conscience. Any deviation, such as Sheila Cloney's challenge to the Catholic Church's *Ne Temere* decree, which prescribed that Protestants had no choice in educating their children as they saw fit, was met with a choleric response.

Neither was Fethard-on-Sea an isolated outbreak of sectarianism. Local intimidation and boycotts of Protestants and the destruction of Protestant-owned property was common in many parts of the country during the War of Independence and Civil War in the early 1920s. In June 1921, a band of over thirty armed men shot dead two young Protestant men in Coolacrease in County Offaly. Fourteen Protestant men, aged between sixteen and eighty-two, were massacred in the Bandon valley in west Cork in April 1922 in revenge for the death of an IRA man. In the Mayo librarian case of 1931, the county library service was boycotted because the Local Appointments Commission appointed a Protestant as county librarian. A further brief, if exceedingly unpleasant, burst of anti-Protestant feeling took place in various parts of the country in response to pogroms against Catholics in Northern Ireland in 1935. In the worst of the incidents, an anti-Protestant mob ran amok in Limerick, smashing the windows of Protestant businesses and churches. In other parts of the country, shots were fired outside Protestant churches, sectarian slogans were painted across walls in villages and threatening letters were sent to Protestant homes. In later years, a sense of denial overtook the communities in which these sectarian incidents occurred – similar to that which continues to this day in Fethard. Many still refuse to acknowledge the existence of a boycott in 1957. This is despite the fact that in 1998 the Catholic Bishop of Ferns, Brendan Comiskey, asked forgiveness for 'the offence and hurt caused to the Church of Ireland community and others by members of my own church, particularly by some of its leaders, in what has become known as the Fethard-on-Sea boycott'.

The Fethard boycott was shaped by the violent and bitter history of the Hook region but also by the hard, sullen 1950s. In many respects Ireland in 1957 was closer to the Ireland of the late nineteenth century than the optimistic country that tentatively emerged in the latter half of the 1960s. At the end of the 1950s, the country was beginning to pull itself slowly out of a long period of economic stagnation, but in 1957 it was still stuck in first gear. The bungalow and motor car had yet to replace the broken-down cottage and the horse and cart. Poverty was endemic. The economy was in tatters. The last time the emigration figures had been so bad was in the late nineteenth century. Those who were not leaving the country were leaving the land, heading to the towns and cities in search of work. The romantic de Valeran dreams of self-sufficiency had failed to come true. The

Introduction

politicians were suitably chastened by the electorate: after sixteen uninterrupted years of Fianna Fáil, there had been four changes of government between 1948 and 1957. Despite the hollow old nationalist rhetoric, no democratic party looked any closer to solving the problem of partition. Instead, it was back to the bullet and the bomb as the IRA launched the Border Campaign against police barracks, customs posts and electricity substations in Northern Ireland in December 1956. The huge attendance at the Limerick funeral of Seán South, the IRA volunteer killed during a raid on an RUC barracks in Fermanagh on New Year's Day 1957, showed that there was still an appetite for old-fashioned 'republican' martyrdom.

It also seemed to be business as usual for the Catholic Church. Priests submitted their parishioners to endless apoplectic homilies about the threat of atheistic Communism. Frequent topics included the imprisonment of Cardinal Mindszenty, the Primate of Hungary; the Soviet Union's ruthless suppression of the uprising in that country in October 1956; and the fate of Irish Catholic missionaries in Chinese jails. A proposed soccer match between Ireland and Yugoslavia was abandoned in 1952 as a protest at the Communist regime. The lead story of the weekly Catholic newspaper *The Standard* (later the *Catholic Standard*) of 10 May 1957 was indicative of the Church-inspired hysteria:

IRISH REDS STILL ACTIVE – LEADERS TRAINED
   IN SOVIET RUSSIA
There are about 700 Communist Party members in Dublin, led by 20 men trained in Leningrad and Moscow. The Reds are 'very interested' in Ireland, and

to meet the threat of their insidious methods now being used, the Bishop of Derry this week called for 'a militant Catholicism from every individual'.

'Impure' books, newspapers, magazines and movies and the dangers they presented to Irish chastity were perceived as another threat to the moral safety of the faithful. The clergy appointed good Catholics to parish vigilance committees to protect the morals of the local citizenry. Committee members would search the public libraries for 'dirty' books and prowl the dance halls and country lanes searching for courting couples. This was an Ireland where intellectual pursuits were actively discouraged, where too much education was frowned upon as being a waste of time. John McGahern, that most perceptive observer of Irish internal and external lives in the 1950s and 1960s, remembers a country where reading for pleasure was thought to be dangerous.

> Time was filled by necessary work, always exaggerated: sleep, Gaelic football, prayer, gossip, religious observance, the giving of advice – ponderously delivered, and received in stupor – civil war politics, and the eternal business that Proust describes as 'Moral Idleness'. This was confined mostly to the new emerging classes – civil servants, policemen, teachers, tillage inspectors. The ordinary farming people went about their sensible pagan lives as they had done for centuries, seeing all this as one of the many veneers they had to pretend to wear, like all the others they had worn since the time of the druids.[1]

Introduction

The self-appointed moral guardians were not confined to the countryside. They were active in the cities' cinemas and theatres too. In May 1957, Alan Simpson, the co-director of the small Pike Theatre in Dublin, was arrested and jailed overnight on the grounds of indecency. What caused offence? One of the actors in a production of Tennessee Williams' *The Rose Tattoo* had pretended to drop a condom on stage.

Catholic devotion took place in public in 1950s' Ireland. Being a good Irishman was inextricably linked to being a good Catholic. The people erected grottoes to the Virgin Mary on urban housing estates, in rural villages and at holy sites in the middle of the countryside throughout the Marian year of 1954. The priest had exclusive moral authority. To go 'agin' him took courage; the priest went to the front of the queue in the shop. The priest was given the best chair in the house. You did not say 'no' to the priest. In this intellectually arid climate, it was easier to conform. To say no had all sorts of implications, metaphysically and socially. Condemnation from the pulpit was dreaded.

Again, McGahern cannot be bettered: 'People did not live in Ireland then. They lived in small, intense communities, and the communities could vary greatly in spirit and character, even over a distance of a few miles.'[2] If there is one incident that sums up the claustrophobic, deeply conservative nature of small-town life in 1950s' rural Ireland, it is the Fethard-on-Sea boycott. The boycott did not cause a seismic shift in Irish society, though the writer Hubert Butler believed passionately that Fethard was a seminal moment for both Catholics and Protestants. But the country did begin to change after 1957.

The Fethard-on-Sea Boycott

In 1958, the Secretary of the Department of Finance, T. K. Whitaker, published *Economic Development*, a groundbreaking study which re-imagined Ireland's economic future as moving away from the protectionist dogma of her adolescence to a more self-confident adulthood willing to take its place in the world – the country had joined the United Nations in 1955 – and adopting free trade and greater liberalisation. In 1959, Éamon de Valera, struggling with blindness, passed the baton to his heir apparent, Seán Lemass. Lemass did not represent the next generation, but was rather a transitional figure, a reassuring figure to allay the fears of the Old Guard – the men who had stuck with the Chief through thick and thin and could rest easy in the knowledge that the revolutionary generation was still in place. But he inaugurated a period of great change in the country. During his brief tenure as Taoiseach, he created the conditions for Irish economic growth and a more mature relationship between the Republic and Northern Ireland. But this was in the future. During that long hot summer of 1957, the country was in paralysis, trying to look forward but being pulled back into the past. The old certainties had yet to be forsaken, and those who had the most to lose were hanging on grimly to the comforts of history.

1

Cromwell's Legacy

A despondent James II stood on Irish soil for the last time at Duncannon Fort on the west coast of the Hook Peninsula on a summer's day in 1690 before he sailed into exile in France. A few days previously the deposed Catholic monarch's last hopes of restoration to the thrones of England, Scotland and Ireland had been crushed at the Battle of the Boyne by his Protestant rival, William of Orange, now William III of England, Scotland and Ireland. A nineteenth-century representation of the scene portrays James as a lonely figure being helped down the steps of the pier at Duncannon. A rowing boat is waiting to take him to his ship anchored in the distance. He is clad from head to foot in black.

The Irish Catholic gentry was in mourning at the end of the seventeenth century. James' defeat meant their hopes of being restored to their former positions of power and influence were dead. Protestants would now govern Ireland for themselves. The body of legislation that became known as the Penal Laws placed harsh restrictions on Catholics' political and religious freedom. It marked the final humili-ation of the native Catholic landowning class who, over the course of 150 years, had seen their economic and political power wiped out by the confiscation and transferral of their estates – firstly under the Tudors and then under the Stuarts and Cromwell – to a new breed of English and Scottish, and more importantly Protestant, landowner who were rewarded for their military service, their own shrewd financial speculations and their loyalty to the English Crown.

It was fitting that James embarked on the first stage of his final voyage into exile from the Hook. From the air, the Hook resembles an elongated forearm punching its way into the sea. As Catholic schoolchildren throughout the country were once taught, it was here, at Bannow Bay, that Ireland's 600 years of suffering at the hands of perfidious Albion had begun. In fact, there were no English aboard the three ships that landed at Bannow Island in 1169. They were a mixture of Normans, Flemings and Welsh under the command of the Norman lord Robert FitzStephen. But history in the hands of nation-builders has to be simple. It needs heroes and villains. And one of the greatest villains of Irish history was the Gaelic chieftain Dermot MacMurrough who, after being ousted as King of Leinster by Tiernan O'Rourke, invited the restless Norman barons from Wales to assist him regain his throne and challenge Rory O'Connor, the High King of Ireland, and in doing so, helped to begin the Norman colonisation of Ireland.

The Normans' first colony was in south Wexford. The evidence of their strong presence in this part of the country are the castles, towns and churches dotted across the landscape and the preponderance of Norman surnames: names such as Stafford, Devereux, Butler and Colfer. The south Wexford colony became a bulwark of their power in Ireland. It was strategically vital to control the Hook because the peninsula guarded the approach to Waterford Harbour and the confluence of the rivers Nore, Barrow and Suir, also known as the Three Sisters, one of the most important river systems in the country. From here, ships could penetrate deep into the rich agricultural hinterland of Leinster and Munster. The Vikings had recognised the harbour's importance by founding their first Irish city at Waterford. The Normans likewise founded New Ross at the confluence of the Barrow and the Nore, just north of the Hook Peninsula, at the beginning of the thirteenth century. The Normans divided the Hook into three monastic estates in order to ensure control. The Cistercians founded the abbeys of Dunbrody and Tintern on lands granted to them in the northeast and northwest of the peninsula. The Norman monarch King Henry II – who arrived in Ireland in 1171 to keep an eye on the growing power of his subjects and claim the Lordship of Ireland – granted the southern part of the Hook, the manor of Kilcloggan, to the Knights Templar, the military monastic order, an indication of the importance he attached to the security of the region. Despite their military superiority, the Normans did not succeed in subjugating the whole of Ireland; coloniser and native settled into a pattern of sporadic skirmishing. The Normans protected themselves from the depredations of the Irish by building great fortified castles made of stone and erecting walls around their towns. New Ross, which soon became one of the most important seaports on the island, lay astride the border of the old Gaelic Ireland and the new Norman colony. The Norman inhabitants of New Ross built an ambitious programme of defensive fortifications to protect themselves from the attacks of Gaelic clans such as the Kennedys and the MacMurroughs.

After centuries of wrestling with the native Irish, the descendants of the great Norman barons gradually settled into a form of cohabitation with their erstwhile enemies. By the beginning of the sixteenth century, the cultural and political demarcation between Norman coloniser and Gaelic native had ceased to exist. The descendants of the original Norman families, or Old English as they were known, famously became more Irish than the Irish themselves, intermarrying and adopting many aspects of Gaelic culture, including language and dress.

The Old English elite nominally governed Ireland at the behest of the Crown. In fact, its authority did not extend beyond the Pale. Outside the Pale, power rested with Gaelic or Old English magnates. Thus royal influence was minimal. This state of affairs changed at the beginning of the sixteenth century. The discovery of the American continent by Columbus in 1492 meant the deep-water ports of Ireland, including Waterford Harbour, became critical staging posts, as the great powers of England, France and Spain vied for control of the Atlantic routes to the rich pickings of the New World. The English Crown, fearful of the threat of invasion from foreign powers, moved to strengthen its hold on Ireland. The Gaelic and Old English lords, jealous of their own power, rose in rebellion, only to be brutally crushed by the Tudor monarch Henry VIII.

Cromwell's Legacy

Then a fatal new element was added to the political situation: religion. Henry's break with Rome and the establishment of the Church of England resulted in a choice in Ireland of adopting the new reformed religion or staying loyal to the old faith. The majority of both the Gaelic and Old English lords chose the latter and, in doing so, laid the foundations for their ultimate political and economic demise. The shift in power on the Hook from the Old English elite to a new class of loyal English Protestant began in 1536 with the dissolution of the monasteries. In that year, the Cistercian estates of Dunbrody and Tintern were suppressed and subsequently granted to two of Henry's trustworthy Protestant soldiers. Sir Osborne Etchingham, a cousin of Anne Boleyn and marshal of the English army in Ireland, successfully petitioned for the grant of the lands at Dunbrody in exchange for lands he held in England. Anthony Colclough, who was later knighted by Elizabeth I, was granted the lands at Tintern.

Some of the Old English, such as the former abbot of Dunbrody, Alexander Devereux, had no apparent difficulty in changing religious allegiance depending on which way the political wind was blowing. Upon the suppression of the monasteries, Devereux became the first Bishop of Ferns in the new Reformed Church. But once the Catholic Mary I ascended the throne of England, he abjured the heresy of the new religion and reverted to Catholicism. When the Protestant Elizabeth I succeeded Mary, he speedily switched sides once again. It is believed that Devereux is buried in St Mogue's Church in Fethard, and that he brought from Dunbrody the baptismal font still used by the Church of Ireland parishioners today.

The Fethard-on-Sea Boycott

For the majority of the Old English and Gaelic landowning families, though, the religious and political upheavals of the sixteenth and seventeenth centuries were catastrophic. A new centralised English administration replaced the power of the Old English gentry. The Old English tried to negotiate with the English Crown to retain their ancient rights and privileges but their loyalty to the old religion was beginning to preclude them from influence. A more radical Protestantism was on the rise across the Irish Sea and, indeed, in Ireland. New settlers from England and Scotland arrived in the country – mostly in the northeast – throughout the early part of the early seventeenth century as part of an ambitious project of plantation designed to strengthen the Protestant interest – and by extension loyalty to the English crown. By the early 1600s, most of the Hook was in the hands of Protestant landlords.

In 1641, a small group of Gaelic Irish landowners, fearful of an impending invasion of Ireland by anti-Catholic forces in Scotland and England, rose in rebellion in Ulster. There were widespread massacres of new English and Scottish Protestant settlers. After years of trying to negotiate with an English Crown, which had continually disenfranchised them, robbed them of their lands and treated them with contempt, the Old English gentry, initially suspicious of the rising, threw in their lot with the Gaelic Irish. This loose alliance, with its headquarters in Kilkenny, was christened the Catholic Confederation. The Confederates took advantage of the Civil War raging in England between Roundhead and Royalist to gain control of the country. The rebellion had become a war.

Cromwell's Legacy

In southwest Wexford, New Ross declared for the Confederation. The Old English families who had seen their political and economic power wane were eager to restore their fortunes. Religion was now becoming a defining feature of political allegiance. Protestants and Catholics sought shelter from the violence on the Hook where they could. Protestant refugees banged on the doors of the garrison at Duncannon Fort. Catholics sought protection behind the sturdy stone walls of the Norman-built castles of their kinsmen. Reprisals were common. Soldiers from Duncannon hanged eighteen Confederates after a raid on Ramsgrange Castle. Under the command of Colonel John Devereux, the Confederates took Tintern Abbey, which was sheltering about 200 Protestants under the protection of 30 soldiers from Duncannon Fort. Fethard also became a Confederate base. In 1645, the Confederate general Thomas Preston gained control of Duncannon Fort. The fort, commanding the narrow approach to Waterford Harbour and the ports of Waterford and New Ross, was again of vital strategic significance because of the renewed threat of foreign invasion by the Catholic powers in Europe.

The expectations raised among the Catholics of south Wexford by the capture of Duncannon Fort were extinguished within five years. In 1649, upon the end of the English Civil War, the Parliamentary general Oliver Cromwell turned his attention to Ireland. After landing in Dublin, Cromwell swept north towards Drogheda, where his massacre of the town's defenders and civilians gave warning to other Confederate garrisons of what was to come if they did not yield. Cromwell then turned south and swept along the eastern seaboard towards Wexford town, where he wreaked bloody retribution on the inhabitants for their perceived treason. The town was burned, the harbour destroyed and hundreds of townspeople were killed during the sack. The inhabitants of New Ross, fearful of what might happen to them should they stand and fight, quickly submitted to the Cromwellian army. After fierce resistance, Waterford and Duncannon also succumbed. Cromwell had achieved his aim. By 1653, through brutal conquest, he had cowed the country into submission. Ireland was shattered by more than a decade of violent warfare. Traumatised Catholic landowners were penalised. Their lands were confiscated, leaving them with little but deep resentment towards the new class of English Protestant soldier and adventurer who had dispossessed them.

Their hopes were briefly reignited by the restoration of Charles II and the Stuart dynasty to the throne in 1660. But by 1688 the aggressively pro-Catholic policies of Charles' successor, James II, had disturbed the Protestant establishment in England to such an extent that James was deposed and the Dutch Prince of Orange, William, was invited to ascend the throne. Two years later, the final Catholic monarch of England failed in his last-ditch effort to regain his crown, and the Battle of Aughrim a year afterwards, in 1691, marked the end of the Jacobite cause in Ireland. But while James resigned himself to his fate, living out his days in luxury in France at the court of the Sun King, Louis XIV, the Catholic gentry continued to dream of the day when the great tragedy that had befallen them during the previous century would be undone.

2

Forgetting Scullabogue

The men being held in the farmhouse at Scullabogue were the first to be killed. They were taken out in groups of four, made to kneel down on the grass and then shot. Women picking at the clothes of the dead for valuables were told to move out of the line of fire as the next batch of men were dispatched. The rest of the prisoners, who were being held in a barn close by, must have quaked in fear as they listened to the shots. There were women and children among their number. Their anxiety turned to terror when burning pieces of straw were thrown into the barn. Then the roof of the barn started to flame. Their desperate attempts to escape were repelled by their captors, who used pikes to keep the prisoners trapped inside. Only four prisoners managed to escape. Scores more died, suffocated by the thick smoke that filled the barn.

Most of those who died during that June morning in 1798 were Protestants. They were being held by a small guarding party at the main rebel camp under Carrigbyrne Hill while the bulk of the rebel army was attempting to capture New Ross, about eight miles away. Historians have debated the motives of the killers. Were they purely sectarian, or were the victims killed because of their political sympathies? Had the guarding party at Scullabogue heard of the rebels' defeat at New Ross and been instructed to kill the prisoners? Or had they acted on their own initiative, driven by bloodlust and a thirst for vengeance? Sir Richard Musgrave, the author of the classic loyalist account of the rebellion published shortly after 1798, was in no doubt.

> Some persons have contended that the persecutions in the country of Wexford were not exclusively levelled against Protestants, because a few Romanists were put to death in the barn and at Wexford; but the sanguinary spirit against them was so uniform at Vinegar-hill, on the bridge of Wexford, and Scullabogue, and indeed in every part of the county, as to remove any doubt on that head.[1]

The later nineteenth-century representation of the massacre, complete with typical stock simian caricatures of the rebels by Dickens' illustrator George Cruikshank, no doubt reinforced the anti-Irish prejudices of many English.

History is written by the victors, however, and in the newly independent Irish State, Scullabogue was quietly ignored. The nationalist version of 1798 was a glorious, if ultimately failed, attempt to cast off the yoke of British rule through the coming together of Catholic, Protestant and

Forgetting Scullabogue

Dissenter led by heroic Catholic priests. The writer Colm
Tóibín grew up in 1960s' Enniscorthy. He remembers how
proud his community was of its links to 1798 but also its
peculiar cultural amnesia:

> The names of the towns and villages around us were in
> all the songs about 1798 – the places where battles had
> been fought, or atrocities committed. But there was
> one place that I did not know had a connection with
> 1798 until I was in my twenties. It was Scullabogue.
> Even now, as I write the name, it has a strange
> resonance. In 1798 it was where 'our side' took a large
> number of Protestant men, women and children, put
> them in a barn and burned them to death.[2]

During the bicentennial commemorations of 1798,
Scullabogue reared its ugly head once again in a debate
carried out in the columns of the national newspapers about
the nature of the Rising in Wexford. None of the ever-
present questions was decisively answered. Official Ireland
quietly drew a veil over the more contentious aspects of the
Rising. The government was keen to promote a non-
sectarian narrative of 1798 at a particularly sensitive stage
in the Northern Ireland peace process.

Whatever about modern cultural sensitivities, it is true
to say that intense sectarian tensions existed in Wexford
during the latter part of the eighteenth century, exacerbated
by the rabid pro-Protestant ascendancy and anti-Catholic
politics of the Loftus family, the predominant political force
in the county, whose power derived from the land it owned
on the Hook. Adam Loftus was the first of the family to

arrive in Ireland from Yorkshire during the reign of Elizabeth I. He was typical of his breed, an Elizabethan opportunist in Ireland hungry for wealth and influence, and with few moral qualms about how to achieve them. Loftus had been raised a Catholic but had switched to Protestantism at an early age. He became Archbishop of Dublin and then the first provost of the newly founded Trinity College. Dudley Loftus, Adam's son, established the family on the Hook, acquiring the former monastic estate at Kilcloggan at the end of the sixteenth century. During the latter part of the seventeenth century they lived in the Norman castle in Fethard. But about 1700, they moved a few miles south to the remote Redmond Hall (later Loftus Hall) close to Hook Head, as if to ready themselves for their spectacular political advancement over the course of the next 100 years.

In 1751, Nicholas Loftus was created Baron Loftus of Loftus Hall and five years later Viscount Loftus of Ely. His elder son, also named Nicholas, was raised to the Earldom of Ely in 1766, a few days before his death. His brother Henry was even more successful, elevating the Loftuses into a separate party in the House of Commons. The basis for this political success was control of eight pocket or 'rotten' boroughs in the county. Bannow, which both Henry and his brother Nicholas represented in the Commons, was little more than 'a mountain of sand, without a single inhabited house'.[3] Unfortunately for the Loftuses, they were incapable of producing male heirs and their estates passed through marriage to the Tottenham family. The Tottenhams, who along with the Leigh family controlled New Ross, were zealous defenders of the Protestant ascendancy in the Irish parliament. Their ultra-loyalist politics sprang from their deep-rooted fear of the barbarians at the gate, the Catholic rabble seeking to usurp them both from within and from without the city walls. In 1730, Charles Tottenham, the sovereign of the town – a position dating from medieval times, the incumbent being elected by members of the New Ross corporation – on behalf of the Protestant inhabitants of the town, petitioned the Lords Justices in Dublin for the repair of the barracks and the retention of the garrison. His reason was that 'the inhabitants of the said towne and the country adjoining being for the greater part most violent Papists, part of the Army's being quartered therein is a great security of the Protestant Interest of that part of the Kingdom'.[4]

The descendants of the Catholic gentry, now largely middlemen or merchants, looked on bitterly from the political sidelines in south Wexford. Disenfranchised and stripped of their lands, they spent the early part of the century in crisis. Their chances of regaining their lands had faded with the dream of a Jacobite restoration. Pro-ascendancy families such as the Loftuses and the Tottenhams, ever nervous of rebellion and invasion and jealous of their political power, were determined to protect their own interests by trampling on Catholic aspirations.

As the century progressed, this Catholic middle class grew in confidence. They opposed trade restrictions placed upon them by the Protestant corporation in New Ross. Their exclusion from the Protestant 'club' led them to found their own confraternities, sodalities and charitable societies. But, despite their growing confidence, these Catholic middlemen and merchants continued to harbour a vitriolic hatred of the ascendancy class and were 'obsessed, almost to the point of neurosis, with ancestry, family background and the Cromwellian rupture'.[5] This economic and political frustration was mirrored further down the social scale. The rapid growth of the population meant intense competition for land. There was less tillage land available as Protestant landlords moved towards the more profitable activity of grazing. Rents climbed, while poor Catholic labourers and tenant farmers shouldered the burden of paying for the established Anglican Church, many of whose absentee rectors rendered no services to the communities that were paying for them. In reaction, oath-bound secret societies, such as the Whiteboys – who got their name from the white smocks they wore to recognise each other in the dark – emerged. These small farmers and labourers would assemble at night to level ditches enclosing common grazing land, dig up pasture land, search houses for arms and attack tithe collectors. In southwest Wexford, the small Protestant enclave at Old Ross was a repeated target of Whiteboy attacks throughout the 1760s and 1770s.

This discontent exploded in the summer of 1798. In the early 1790s, inspired by Enlightenment ideas, the Anglican lawyer Theobald Wolfe Tone had founded the Society of United Irishmen in Belfast with the aim of achieving greater political representation for Presbyterians and Catholics. In the space of a few years, the United Irishmen had become an underground revolutionary organisation dedicated to overthrowing British rule in Ireland. Its leaders sought to persuade the Revolutionary French Directory to provide help for a rebellion. The United Irishmen hoped to harness the discontented Catholic tenants to the rebellion and used ballads and poems to bring their message to the rural peasantry, often associating their ideas with the old Jacobite cause. In southwest Wexford, where the Irish language was still strong, oral culture held out the promise of the return of the Stuarts and the overturning of the hated Cromwellian land settlement. Prosperous Wexford Catholics and those lower down the social scale with economic grievances were drawn to the United Irish message. While the rebellion in Dublin ended in dismal failure on the night of 23 May 1798, the popular rising in Wexford was initially successful. By the end of the month, most of the county, including Wexford town and Enniscorthy, was in rebel hands. Encouraged by these initial military successes, recruits flocked to the rebel army. At the beginning of June, the bulk of this rebel army was camped on Carrigbyrne Hill preparing for an attack on nearby New Ross. The town was important not only strategically – allowing the rebels to break west out of Wexford towards Waterford and the rest of Munster – it was a bitter symbol of Protestant supremacy. Most of the rebels camped on the hill were locals. Many would go back home every couple of days to sleep. Others used the opportunity to settle old scores. While waiting for the attack on New Ross to begin, raiding parties from the rebel camp at Carrigbyrne scoured the countryside for prisoners. Their efforts were focused on the small Protestant enclaves at Fethard, Tintern and Old Ross.

Michael Devereux, a Catholic middleman, and Joshua Colfer, a maltster, led parties through Fethard several times during late May and early June in search of prisoners. Devereux was from Battlestown, a couple of miles north of Fethard. The large Devereux connection had formerly been one of the most prominent landowning families in south Wexford. Indeed, Devereux's family still held as middlemen the 600 acres that they had lost in the previous century. Colfer, on the other hand, was employed by a Protestant brewer in Fethard. Another rebel, John Houghran, a stonemason from Tintern, similarly returned home to search for Protestant neighbours. The historian Daniel Gahan points out the economic motives for their actions:

> If we consider the political and sectarian symbolism of such communities, and the likelihood that economic rivalry surely developed between craftsmen and labourers of both religions in their vicinity, then it is not surprising that Catholic artisans and labourers would be active in the campaign against such people.[6]

Protestant witnesses, some the widows of prisoners killed at Scullabogue, testified later that the rebels ordered them to be baptised by a Catholic priest.

The rebels were particularly anxious to find the whereabouts of members of the Hornick family. The Hornicks had arrived in Wexford at the beginning of the eighteenth century. They were part of a wave of Protestant refugees who had fled the Rhine Palatinate region of modern-day Germany because of famine, plague and religious persecution. The British monarch Queen Anne had offered political asylum to these Palatine families and several were settled in Ireland, mainly in Limerick. The Hornicks were among a group settled on the estate of the Ram family at Old Ross and Killann in Wexford. The Rams gave their new tenants good land at low rents, which led to much resentment among their Catholic neighbours who were treated a lot less favourably. The Hornicks became particularly unpopular for their unashamed loyalist leanings. George Hornick was known as a Whiteboy hunter. In 1775, he had beaten off a Whiteboy attack on his house at Killann, killing one of the attackers. He subsequently founded a defence league against Whiteboyism, marching to church on Sundays under arms. This provoked his Catholic neighbours. 'That event excited the most implacable vengeance in the breasts of those ferocious fanatics, against this loyal but unfortunate family,' wrote the admittedly biased Musgrave about the repercussions of the 1775 Whiteboy attack.[7] The Hornicks suffered dearly during the Rising in Wexford. As many as seven of the family may have been killed during early June, including Philip Hornick, who was shot at Scullabogue, and two of his nephews. Fr Philip Roche, one of the foremost clerical leaders of the rebellion in Wexford, led a raid on the Hornick homestead at Killann, a few miles west of Enniscorthy in the shadow of the Blackstairs Mountains. The Palatine families in Old Ross were luckier in that most of them had escaped to the comparative safety of New Ross or Waterford. However, the rebels took their revenge by burning the village to the ground, including the Protestant church.

The Palatine families who were burnt out were slow to return to County Wexford after the rebellion had been stamped out. But just over seventy years later, Robert Hornick, a manager at Denny's bacon factory in Waterford, bought the lease of 43 acres of land at John's Hill just outside Fethard village from a poor Catholic farmer, Nicholas Murphy, and his son, James. The new owner must have been content with his purchase. John's Hill was good land. Others were less pleased that such a prime piece of land had shifted from Catholic to Protestant hands. Not only was a Protestant snapping up the land from a Catholic family that had fallen into difficulty – a very great sin in the eyes of many of the villagers – but the Protestant in question was from a family remembered locally as being anti-Catholic loyalists. There were long memories on the Hook. And many of the Catholics vowed that they would not let another scrap of land slip through their fingers.

3

Learning how to Boycott

In September 1886 a large group of tenant farmers
gathered on the pier at Ballyhack on the western side of
the Hook to board the steamship which would bring them
across the water to the market at Waterford. As the farmers
were clambering aboard with their goods, two latecomers
arrived at the pier accompanied by a couple of RIC men.
Godfrey Taylor and his wife were well known to their fellow
passengers. Taylor was the hated land agent for the Marquis
of Ely, the absentee owner of the former Loftus (now Ely)
estate. As Taylor and his wife proceeded on board with the
two policemen, the other passengers began to disembark and
unload their goods. Those still on the quayside signalled that
they were refusing to embark and travelled to Waterford
instead in a number of fishing boats.[1] A few days later the
scene was repeated at the quays in Waterford. Taylor and his
wife arrived on board the steamer to be greeted with a low
murmur from the farmers returning to the Hook. Within a

few minutes all the passengers on board had disembarked except for a couple of soldiers and their wives. While those around him hurriedly grabbed their possessions and left in protest at his presence, Taylor sat quietly smoking his pipe and reading a newspaper, his back to the quay. As the steamer set off, again with only a handful on board, the large crowd on the quay began to groan and shout. Taylor slowly rose from his seat, briefly turning to face his tormentors before the ship pulled away from the quays.[2] The boycott of Taylor was the result of a heated campaign for tenants' rights on the Hook orchestrated over five years by the parish priest of Ramsgrange, Canon Thomas Doyle, and an extraordinary curate by the name of David O'Hanlon Walsh.[3]

At the end of the 1870s, owing to a poor harvest, the third in succession, and a depression in agricultural prices in Britain brought about by cheap American imports, thousands of poor tenant farmers were being evicted from their homesteads for non-payment of rent by mostly Protestant landlords unwilling to take into account their reduced circumstances. Poverty and agrarian violence blighted the countryside. Against this backdrop, thousands of tenant farmers attended a monster meeting in Irishtown in County Mayo, one of the worst-afflicted parts of the country, in April 1879. Five months later the Irish National Land League was founded in Castlebar with Charles Stewart Parnell as president and Michael Davitt as one of its honorary secretaries. The aims of the new organisation were an end to excessive rents, or rack rents, and the ultimate ownership of the land by those who worked it. During the next twelve months, branches of the Land League sprang up across Ireland.

Learning how to Boycott

In September 1880 tenant farmers on the Erne estate in Mayo demanded a reduction in their rents. The estate's agent, Captain Charles Boycott, refused and began evicting tenants. In response, the local Land League began a campaign of ostracising the agent, which became so effective that the word 'boycott' entered the English language. By November, the London *Times* was using the notorious agent's name for the new campaign adopted by the League and outlined by Parnell in a famous speech in Ennis:

> When a man takes a farm from which another has been evicted, you must show him on the roadside when you meet him, you must show him in the streets of the town, you must show him at the shop-counter, you must show him in the fair and at the marketplace, and even in the house of worship, by leaving him severely alone, by putting him into a sort of moral Coventry, by isolating him from the rest of his kind as if he were a leper of old, you must show him your detestation of the crime he has committed, and you may depend upon it if the population of a county in Ireland carry on this doctrine, that there will be no man so full of avarice, so lost to shame, as to dare the public opinion of all right-thinking men within the county and to transgress your unwritten code of laws.[4]

In August 1880 a letter writer to the nationalist Wexford newspaper, the *People*, wondered: 'Sir, The Irish National Land League is now assuming such dimensions, spreading itself throughout the country, that it is a matter of some comment, why it is, that the "Model" county is so backward in the good cause . . .'[5] Soon the campaign was up and running. Six weeks later 30,000 attended a Land League rally in New Ross. The *People* devoted four pages to the meeting, which was attended by Parnell, describing it as 'one of the largest demonstrations, if not actually the largest, ever held in the county'.[6] Land League branches were organised throughout the county over the coming months.

The Catholic clergy were the driving force behind the local organisation of the League. In County Wexford there was a tradition of hero priests. Every Catholic schoolchild in Wexford knew about the exploits of Fr John Murphy who was killed fighting the Crown forces during the 1798 Rising. In the aftermath of Catholic Emancipation in 1829 and the Great Famine of the 1840s, priests had become the natural leaders of rural communities. Members of the rural clergy generally came from the more prosperous tenant farming and trading families – those who had survived the desolation of the Famine – who could afford to have their sons educated. This rural middle class was the power base of the resurgent late nineteenth-century Catholic Church. It was the farmers and shopkeepers who paid for the churches, schools, hospitals and orphanages that the Church built with such vigour during the thirty or so years after 1850. As the institutional Church grew in confidence during the latter part of the nineteenth century under the leadership of a series of dynamic prelates, the clergy, with the financial and moral support of the strong farmers and the professional and merchant classes, became the mobilisers of their communities, and now headed the local campaigns for agrarian reform.

In October 1880 the parish priest of Ramsgrange, Canon

Learning how to Boycott

Thomas Doyle, organised a meeting after Sunday Mass for the purpose of starting a local branch of the Land League. The branch would cover the tenantry of the Templemore, Ely and Colclough estates or the three Catholic parishes on the Hook. His experience of working as a young curate in the fever sheds of New Ross during the Famine had had a profound impact on Thomas Doyle and he had long been a champion of tenants' rights in south Wexford. Speaking in the chapel yard in Ramsgrange that Sunday on the 'burning question of the land', Canon Doyle told his parishioners that 'the only settlement which he considered eminently satisfactory and certainly final was occupying ownership, so that every farmer could say of the land on which he expended his sweat and toil – "this is my own, the fruits of my labour and toil, and for myself and my children and my children's children"'. At this early stage, Doyle believed that the tenants could strengthen Parnell by 'uniting together in legal combinations, and by constitutional agitation'.[7] It was an implicit rejection of violence.

While Doyle was rousing his parishioners on the Hook, on the other side of south Wexford, Fr David O'Hanlon Walsh, the curate in Kilrane, near Rosslare Harbour, was rallying the Catholic tenants with even more fiery speeches. O'Hanlon Walsh, though himself from a prosperous tenant farming family, witnessed desperate poverty growing up in the townland of Knocktartan near Ballymitty in the post-Famine era. His father died when he was young, leaving his mother as the head of the household. Davy, the second son, was educated at St Peter's College in Wexford town, and then studied for the priesthood at the Catholic University of Louvain in Belgium on a scholarship. Following his ordination in 1871, he was appointed to a curacy in Caim near Enniscorthy. From there he was transferred to Tinahely and then to Kilrane.[8] On 17 October 1880, farmers, labourers, shopkeepers and tradesmen gathered in Kilrane to hear O'Hanlon Walsh speak at a meeting to establish a branch of the Land League. The leading tenant farmers of the district sat alongside the curate on a temporary platform, which had been erected for the meeting and above which fluttered a large green flag with the inscription 'Welcome to Parnellstown'. Renaming places and buildings after the leaders and methods of the League was one of O'Hanlon Walsh's favoured tactics. When the curate rose to move to the front of the platform and announced the village's change of name, the crowd let out cries of 'Parnellstown for ever'. The *People* reported that 259 names were enrolled in the local Land League branch that day. A week later, 10,000 people gathered for a meeting in Wellington Bridge organised by Canon Doyle. O'Hanlon Walsh, who had travelled to Wellington Bridge with a group of supporters, was among those who addressed the cheering crowd.

The following month, the campaign in south Wexford took a dramatic turn when the tenants on the scattered south Wexford estates of Colonel Tottenham resolved to pay no more than Griffith's valuation[9] as rent. Tottenham's agent, Thomas Boyd, rejected the tenants' offer, offering instead a 10 per cent reduction in rent to those who paid promptly. It was now the tenants' turn to refuse. The landlord began legal proceedings against the tenants, among them the Walsh family of Knocktartan. But Mary Walsh refused to pay, offering instead what she considered to be a fair rent. This was refused and the sheriff and the bailiff arrived at the farm in Knocktartan with eighty RIC men to evict the family. There was no one at home when they arrived but this did not prevent the police from throwing the family's furniture out on to the road. Fr O'Hanlon Walsh had by now been transferred to the Hook where he was again inspiring the fierce devotion of his hard-pressed parishioners.

On 15 August, the Feast of the Assumption, he led his followers to his family home in Knocktartan. The Walsh family had continued to occupy a barn on the property. A group of emergency men were guarding the farmhouse. An arch spanned the road with mottoes supporting Parnell and saying 'Welcome to the Barn'. O'Hanlon Walsh tried to gain entry to the farmhouse but was refused. Instead, the priest and his supporters moved off towards the nearby village of Taghmon for a Land League meeting, which had been planned for later that day. There, the locals had festooned flags and banners along the street. Another triumphal arch, as was common for celebrations in the late nineteenth century, had been placed across the road. Fifteen thousand people from throughout the county attended the meeting in Taghmon. O'Hanlon Walsh arrived on horseback at the head of a couple of hundred men. This band of followers became known as the Hook 200.

O'Hanlon Walsh's next move was to fire up the Ely tenants on the Hook. In September 1881 the tenants met outside Fethard. They resolved to pay no further rent until rack rents were abolished. The RIC reported that O'Hanlon Walsh had used threatening language at the meeting and announced that watchmen would be appointed to make sure tenants did not attempt to pay rent. Meanwhile,

The Fethard-on-Sea Boycott

O'Hanlon Walsh named the presbytery beside the chapel at Templetown 'Davitt House', after Michael Davitt, while two rows of cottages in Fethard became known as Obstruction Place and Dynamite Row – a provocation to the authorities. O'Hanlon Walsh campaigned frenetically across south Wexford. He condemned the New Ross traders who were supplying the emergency men at Knocktartan, passed resolutions boycotting all sports and amusements associated with landlordism, such as hunting and racing, and endorsed the 'No Rent' manifesto issued by the jailed Land League leaders.[10]

On 13 October, the Walsh family won a victory against Colonel Tottenham at Taghmon petty sessions. Mary Walsh was still living in the barn at Knocktartan. Tottenham had summonsed her, along with her daughter and son, Mary Anne and Nicholas, and two other men, Michael O'Grady and Patrick Lacy, for unlawful trespass. The case was thrown out when it was ruled the defendants had a bona fide belief that they were in possession of the farm and that the sheriff had failed to clear all the stock off the farm.

The authorities in Dublin were beginning to take notice of O'Hanlon Walsh's activities. Reports from the local RIC, the resident magistrate Robert Kennedy, and the object of much of the priest's vitriol, Ely's agent Godfrey Taylor, flooded into Dublin Castle. Taylor wrote to the Chief Secretary, William Edward Forster, telling him the tenants on the Ely estate were afraid to pay their rents because of the edicts of the curate and his band of followers. Not only was he organising the Ely tenantry but he was travelling the countryside organising the tenantry of many of the other nearby south Wexford estates as well. By the end of November, the RIC was recommending that O'Hanlon Walsh be arrested, but the authorities in Dublin Castle realised that this could lead to an outbreak of violence on the Hook.

In April 1882, O'Hanlon Walsh confronted the bailiff during an eviction in Fethard. Again the authorities were loath to arrest him, despite his persistently extreme rhetoric – an example of which were the remarks he made after the sensational murders of the newly appointed Chief Secretary, Lord Frederick Cavendish, and the permanent head of the Irish civil service, the Under Secretary, Thomas Henry Burke, in the Phoenix Park in May that year: 'I have no more sympathy with the victims, Lord Cavendish and Mr Burke, than I would have with a rat.'[11]

The intervention of the Bishop of Ferns, Michael Warren, succeeded in keeping O'Hanlon Walsh quiet for a spell, but the following year the resident magistrate, Kennedy, reported to Dublin Castle that the curate was again making trouble:

Up to the day he was murdered, Mr Burke felt the gravest anxiety about the conduct of a Roman Catholic Priest, the Revd O'Hanlon Walsh, who is stationed in this Diocese. Wherever he has gone, he has done mischief, and for two years, he succeeded in stopping the payment of rents to Lord Ely's property and on every other property to which his mischievous influence extended. Owing to pressure from me on the Bishop, he was interdicted from appearing in public, and this silence was more or less preserved till last Sunday. From the altar on that day, he addressed the

people in the most brutal and incendiary manner – I
think this language must be taken notice of.[12]

A second warning from the bishop was to have the same
effect as the first. O'Hanlon Walsh seems to have tempor-
arily curtailed his involvement with the land agitation
before again inciting his parishioners, notably at a race
meeting on Fethard strand he proclaimed boycotted in
September 1884.

The boycott was the League's[13] most useful tool but it
depended, of course, on collective action. The greatest
scorn was reserved for 'grass grabbers' or those who traded
with boycotted agents. The sanction for those accused of
such crimes was also social and economic ostracism.
Exclusion from the local branch of the League was a de
facto boycott in itself.

O'Hanlon Walsh vented his displeasure at any individual
who disobeyed his instructions. 'I will say no more to that
young man but we will leave him severely alone as God left
the Jews of old,' he told the League after one such individual
had committed an infraction of his instructions. On spotting
a number of men from the nearby parish of Bannow attending
the race meeting on Fethard strand, O'Hanlon Walsh had
'asked them what brought them there or did they not know
that this was a boycotted race. A race to make fun for a
house-burning agent.' He then expounded on his view of
agents: 'They are all bad. Shake them all in a bag and the first
fellow comes out give him a kick for they are all alike. I mean
to sweep them all out of the country – they and landlordism
and then you will have a free country to enjoy the fruits of
your labours.' The curate's unstinting opposition to

landlordism seemed to have stemmed from his childhood experiences: 'I remember a scene when a boy which occurred to my mother. Since then I vowed vengeance against landlordism and the government of this country that while I have strength in my arm to take up a sprong[14] I will ever be at your side to fight for you when required.' The priest, believing his days in the parish were numbered – he told the crowd that he might not be at their next meeting – resorted to increasingly confrontational language. It was as if he was making one last effort to have the authorities arrest him: 'I will speak against land lord repression and when dead my ghost will haunt them just as the ghost of Myles Joyce is haunting Red Jack.'[15] A rumour began spreading through Fethard that the bishop was about to move their curate. O'Hanlon Walsh himself was not unduly concerned, saying 'eight months was enough in any parish'.

> You should be well enough instructed now after four years hard fighting. Combination and determination and you must and will win. You now know what to do and act for yourselves. All grass grabbers and grass snakes must be put out.
>
> I heard there is a fellow after taking Wellington-bridge public house from which the widow Murphy was evicted. Now don't enter that house when going to Wexford to sell your barley. Don't even put your foot inside of it. That is a boycotted house. If you want drink go round by Ross or Fooksmills. The widow Murphy will have that place yet; as Nick [O'Hanlon Walsh's brother, Nicholas] will have Knocktartin; and Pat Neville will have Lewestown.[16]

The Fethard-on-Sea Boycott

After further exchanges with Dublin Castle, Robert Kennedy got an undertaking from the new Bishop of Ferns, James Browne, to move O'Hanlon Walsh from the Hook. Despite a protest of between fifty and eighty of O'Hanlon Walsh's supporters on 2 November 1884, triggered by his resignation as President of the Hook branch of the National League, Bishop Browne duly moved him to Castlebridge, just north of Wexford town.

John Lyng replaced O'Hanlon Walsh as curate. O'Hanlon Walsh's devoted followers were so incensed that the bishop had acceded to the Castle's pressure that, on Lyng's first Sunday in the parish, he was met by a group of about 100 at the parish church, some of whom were carrying pitchforks and shovels. They told him that he would not be allowed to celebrate Mass until O'Hanlon Walsh was reinstated. Kennedy, who was in bed suffering from bronchitis, advised Dublin Castle that if the new priest was to open the chapel, he would need to be protected and 'with a strong force, for the people around that part of the country would stop at no violence, now that their leader has been taken from them'.[17]

During the next two and a half months, there was a stand-off between O'Hanlon Walsh's supporters and the bishop. The parish church was boarded up, as was the presbytery, Davitt Hall, so that the new priest could not say Mass. O'Hanlon Walsh's supporters acquired a new nickname: the former Hook 200 became the Hook Nailors or Hook Chapel Nailors. They posted sentries outside the presbytery and the church and no one was allowed inside. On 17 November 1884, the Nailors assembled outside the chapel. One of them said the rosary and asked for prayers for the sick of the parish. Twelve members of the RIC looked on. The Nailors demanded that no Mass be said and no dues be paid until Fr Davy was restored. The church was constantly watched on Sundays to make sure the parish priest and his new curate did not break the barricade. Each time the curate tried to gain entry to the church by breaking down the boards, they were nailed up again. In place of Mass, one of the Nailors would lead prayers outside the chapel. The bishop managed to resolve the situation only the following February by replacing Lyng with a new curate. A rumour that the parish was to be placed under interdict (meaning that Mass and certain sacraments could not be celebrated in the church) may also have played a part in persuading Fr Davy's supporters to back down.

Despite the departure of O'Hanlon Walsh, 1886/87 saw some of the most bitter and violent scenes of the campaign on the Hook. In August 1886 fifty men, women and children were evicted from their homes in Fethard for non-payment of rent. The National League organised a demonstration in protest. A band played as thousands of men and women accompanied the evicted tenants to the workhouse in New Ross. The nationalist New Ross Board of Guardians, sympathetic to the plight of the evicted tenants, placed a ward at their disposal, which became known as the 'Ward of Honour'. The tenants were not treated as paupers and were not obliged to wear the workhouse clothes. They were given special food and were allowed to receive visitors whenever they wished.[18] The government responded by dissolving the Board of Guardians and appointing vice-guardians, paid by the Local Government Board, in their place. This further alienated nationalist opinion in New

The Fethard-on-Sea Boycott

Ross and south Wexford. A campaign against the payment of the rates was begun and, in response, the vice-guardians reduced the supplies to the workhouse. Relations between the Ely tenantry and the authorities were at a new low. The resignation of the master and the matron of the workhouse did not help matters. On 17 February 1887 the simmering tensions in the workhouse exploded into violence. A bed was set on fire in one of the wards and the next day 200 of the female inmates marched into the boardroom demanding to see the vice-guardians.[19]

The next morning about 100 policemen led by Kennedy arrived to arrest twenty-seven of the workhouse inmates. The women barricaded themselves into the ward to prevent the police from entering. They started shouting as the police tried to smash open the door of the ward. Eventually they managed to break the barricade, only to find the women in bed stripped naked. They laughed at Kennedy and the police when they asked the women to dress themselves. The townspeople threw stones and shouted taunts at Kennedy and the police as they brought the suspects from the workhouse to the courthouse. At one stage the police charged the crowd. Outside the courthouse there was more jeering, especially when the vice-guardians arrived. The case taken by the vice-guardians against the inmates was adjourned after consultations between Kennedy, the police, the vice-guardians and the parish priest, John Kirwan. It was agreed that the case would be dropped if the twenty-seven inmates conducted themselves better during the next week. But this was not enough to quell the crowd waiting outside, some of whom followed the vice-guardians through the streets of New Ross throwing mud at them. Another confrontation between the crowd and the police occurred at the workhouse and one report stated that the inmates seized the van belonging to the workhouse's bread contractor.[20] Order was briefly restored until the following afternoon when the departure of the workhouse matron provoked further unrest among the female inmates of the workhouse who were assembled outside and who 'were loud in their demonstrations of sorrow, many of them being apparently afflicted with too much alcoholic stimulant, which it is believed was passed over the wall to them from outside'.[21]

The Catholic schoolchildren of New Ross also joined in the disturbances. A week after the initial riot in the workhouse, the Christian Brothers boys, about 300 in all, paraded through the streets, before gathering outside the school and demanding that the son of the new workhouse master be put out. They then made their way to the workhouse where they threw stones at the gate. The authorities eventually brought in more police to quell the violence in the town and restore order. Most of the tenants had returned home to Fethard by June. They received a mixed welcome. Some thought they had betrayed the campaign, while others believed they had suffered enough.

The Land War left bitter memories of eviction among the tenants of the Hook and increased the moral power of the local clergy. It had been shown that collective action was the best method of defeating the enemy and that the community's most potent tactic was the boycott. And in 1957, when the Catholic community strove for a swift response to what was perceived as a great injustice, they were able to reach back into the armoury of their collective past and find the weapon they required.

4

Growing up in Fethard

Seán Cloney was seven when he watched his father's
funeral cortège make its way towards the graveyard
at Templetown Church in 1934. Standing in front
of the family home, he could see the long solemn
procession proceed slowly along the narrow road 200
yards away at the bottom of the lane. He could hear his
invalid mother, confined to an upstairs room by
rheumatoid arthritis, sobbing. The scene was to remain
etched on his memory. A glance at an account of the
funeral in the local press gives some idea of the esteem in
which Michael Cloney was held in County Wexford.
Members of the county's professional and business classes,
and representatives and officials of the different public
bodies attended. There were at least sixteen Catholic
priests on the altar and in the choir, an indication of the
Cloney family's standing within the Church. The parish
priest, Canon Thomas Cloney, the deceased's brother,

celebrated Mass. The Church of Ireland rector was also present.

Michael Cloney was an energetic thirty-year-old when he first arrived on the Hook in 1896. From nearby Old Ross, he had been working as a clerk in Dublin when, upon the death of their brother, his three female cousins had invited him to take over the running of the 116-acre farm and mill at Dungulph Castle in Saltmills, about a mile and a half north of Fethard. The first thing Michael Cloney did when he arrived in Dungulph was to restore the old watermill and kiln. Later he began his great project of restoring the dilapidated castle as a residence, buying the property from the Irish Land Commission in 1912 as a tenant purchaser under a 63-year lease.

Michael Cloney remained a bachelor for the first fifty years of his life. But women dominated the household in Dungulph: two of his cousins were widows, the third was a spinster. Given the proprieties of the age, it was inconceivable that Michael Cloney could bring a bride into Dungulph. Instead, he waited until the last of his cousins passed away. His first wife, Elizabeth, died shortly after arriving in the newly restored Dungulph Castle in 1917. She had contracted tetanus when she cut herself while separating butter. Michael Cloney was grief-stricken. Eight years later he married again, this time to Ellen Cavanagh, from a strongly nationalist family who lived near Gorey in the north of the county. Seán, their only child, was born a year later.

Michael Cloney was extremely active in the local community and in Wexford politics. He was a member of the county council, the county agricultural committee and the county library committee. He was a Justice of the Peace under the British and was made a Peace Commissioner by the Irish Free State. One of his proudest achievements was helping to found the local co-operative society, becoming its first chairman in 1919 and serving in that position until his death in 1934. Indeed, it was while on a visit to Dublin as a member of a deputation to the Minister for Agriculture, Jim Ryan, that he was taken ill with pneumonia and admitted to the Mater Hospital. He died there a couple of weeks later. In 1935, at the unveiling of Michael Cloney's headstone, Minister Ryan, who was a family friend from Tomcoole in south Wexford, said: 'We can only imagine what a glorious country we would have if we had in every parish one man with the public spirit, the tact, the ability and the breadth of vision of Michael Cloney.'[1]

Cloney was a man who transcended the feuds and rivalries that govern relations in small rural communities. He remained neutral during the Civil War – though many of his friends were staunch Fianna Fáilers – and was known to enjoy good relations with his Protestant neighbours. Still, he came from strong farmer stock and several of his family were pillars of the Church; his first loyalty was to his own co-religionists.

In 1922, Michael's brother, Thomas, the local parish priest, set up a committee to bid for six acres of land at Fethard Castle, on the edge of the village, which the Ely estate had put up for auction. It was decided that Michael should do the bidding and pay for the property out of his own private funds, should it be knocked down to him. The committee believed that because of Cloney's friendship with his Protestant neighbours, they would not bid against him.

The parish would then reimburse Cloney the price of the property through local fund-raising. The clergy had a strong economic imperative to make sure that the land did not fall into Protestant hands, i.e. the generation of extra income for the parish. There was also a moral imperative for the Catholics in the village – a sense of reclaiming ownership of land that had been stolen from their ancestors by the 'Cromwellians'.

Cloney bought the land for £100. The new legal owners of and trustees for the parish were Michael Cloney, Thomas Cloney, Pat O'Brien and Jim Gleeson. It was envisaged that the land would be turned into a football pitch. But shortly after the land was bought, the Civil War broke out and split the trustees. Pat O'Brien, an unobtrusive local miller, was a key member of the local IRA. It was believed locally that he held large amounts of money for them, including the proceeds of bank raids. In the opposite camp was Jim Gleeson, a farmer who lived next door to Dungulph Castle and who was an ardent admirer of Michael Collins. With the committee divided, the land at the castle was leased to a local farmer, who paid rent to the parish for twenty years. He later bought the land from the parish with the blessing of the Cloney family.

The death of Michael Cloney at the age of sixty-eight was a severe blow to his widow and young son. Running the farm, mill and household at Dungulph was no easy task. Ellen Cloney employed four men to help on the farm. Then there was the miller and his assistant and a couple of women who helped look after the men working outside and run the household. Seán realised that the continuance of the operation at Dungulph depended on him. One day his uncle, the parish priest Thomas Cloney, asked him what he wanted to do with his life now that his father was gone. He replied: 'Carry on here, Canon.'[2] The decision was made. Seán would take over the farm after completing his schooling.

The 1930s were harsh times for farmers. It was nearly impossible to sell cattle on the export market because of the Economic War between Britain and Ireland over de Valera's decision to withhold payment of the land annuities. Farmers who wished to sell cattle abroad had to obtain a licence directly from the Minister for Agriculture for every finished animal. After the death of her husband, Ellen Cloney found herself having to lease the land at Dungulph and sell the livestock until Seán was old enough to take over the running of the farm. This she did successfully, with the exception of ten fat cattle; without the export licences, it would be impossible to get rid of them. So she wrote a letter to the minister, Jim Ryan. Both Michael and Ellen were friends of the Ryan family. Martin, Jim's brother, had been curate in the parish of Templetown until his death in 1923. Jim Ryan had been elected the Sinn Féin deputy for South Wexford in the 1918 general election. Ryan rejected the Treaty and became a senior member of Fianna Fáil upon the foundation of the party in 1926. In 1932, he became Minister for Agriculture in the first Fianna Fáil government, a position he would hold for fifteen years. Ryan was a big, broad man, with the open face of an amiable farmer. But beneath the bluff exterior was a wily political operator. Ryan granted fifteen export licences to Ellen Cloney, five more than she required. Ellen Cloney then sold the cattle to Tommy Kelly, a neighbouring Protestant farmer and cattle dealer.

Growing up in Fethard

Kelly was married to a daughter of William Hornick of John's Hill, just outside Fethard. William Hornick, a close friend of Michael Cloney, was the son of Robert Hornick, who had bought John's Hill in 1870, thus causing the displeasure of many of his Catholic neighbours. William Hornick was one of the local Protestants who would have been in a position to have bid for the land at Fethard Castle. The Cloneys and the Kellys were on good terms. As well as the ten licences Tommy Kelly needed to sell the cattle, Ellen Cloney also gave him the extra five, perhaps in exchange for the good price he gave her. Kelly was known as a charitable man. He was well regarded locally and quick to help a neighbour in need. However, his own charity was not always reciprocated. For many years he had leased a piece of land opposite John's Hill from a poor widow known as Mary Bob. Kelly had believed that if the widow was going to sell the lands it would be to him. Instead the local curate arranged a deal with Pat Neville, the principal of the local national school, whereby he would pay her 2s 6d a week in exchange for the land. It was a tough lesson for Kelly: that Catholic land must be kept in the hands of Catholics at all costs.

While his mother was struggling to manage the farm at Dungulph, eleven-year-old Seán was sent to live with his uncle, the parish priest, for a year. Canon Cloney lived in the parish house beside Templetown Church, a few miles southwest of Fethard on the road to Hook Head. The Pugin-inspired neo-Gothic building, constructed from local sandstone, commands the surrounding countryside, a good example of the triumphalism of the late Victorian Church. For the best part of fifty years, Canon Thomas Cloney was parish priest of Templetown (previously known as Hook parish). A famed and feared figure in both parish and diocese, Cloney had been a classmate at Maynooth of the future Archbishop of Melbourne, Daniel Mannix, and spent time teaching at St Peter's College in Wexford town. In 1911, he became the parish priest at Templetown and later archdeacon and dean, though he was always known as Canon Cloney. Thomas Cloney was an imposing presence around the Hook. Over 17 stone in his prime, he prowled the parish in an 'enormous black tent-like cape, which he fastened around the neck by means of a gold-coloured chain, which reached almost to the ground'.[3] Canon Cloney, as was typical of the Irish Victorian churchman, would not tolerate the slightest impropriety when it came to the meeting of the sexes and had a reputation for giving a clout of his blackthorn to any courting couple who had the misfortune to stray into his path. In his own house, he was loath to intrude on what he regarded as the domain of his housekeeper, the kitchen and pantry, even when she was absent from the house.

According to Seán Cloney, 'Such a presence, coupled with a determined and serious mien, often struck fear and dread into those who met him, so much so that many failed to notice the very humorous twinkle in the eyes behind the gold-rimmed spectacles.'[4] Nevertheless, discipline was strict in the parish priest's house. The Canon expected his nephew to obey the rules. Seán would begin his day serving early morning Mass as an altar boy before cycling the three miles to school. After school, he would cycle back to Templetown where he would do his lessons.

Seán's love of learning was undoubtedly fostered by the year he stayed in the Canon's house. His free time was largely spent reading. The Canon had a large library with many volumes on a range of subjects in English, Irish, French and Latin. Occasionally, uncle and nephew would chat about local history. The Canon was a keen local historian, as had been Michael Cloney. In 1938 the Canon chaired the 1798 commemoration committee and brought Seán to see the long columns of pikemen marching through Wexford town. Seán was to inherit this love of history.

Seán began his secondary education as a boarder, aged twelve, at Rockwell College in County Tipperary. The Canon had wanted him to go to St Peter's College in Wexford but Seán's mother had taken the advice of her solicitor, who had recommended Rockwell. Few families in the area could afford to send their children to secondary school and at home Seán revelled in being a 'college boy'.[5] He admitted to a 'slight feeling of superiority' because of his 'good schooling'. This was many years before the advent of free secondary education in the late 1960s. The number of local boys who were educated beyond national school locally would have been tiny and this would have marked Seán out from his peers. In his first year at Rockwell, Seán developed a love of amateur dramatics when chosen to play the lead in an adaptation of *Little Lord Fauntleroy* by Frances Hodgson Burnett. He was to retain this love of the stage throughout his life. Indeed, there was something of the bohemian about the young Cloney, perhaps a sense of being the outsider. His later adoption of a beret made him stand out in an intensely conservative rural community such as Fethard. Many of his contemporaries would have regarded this break with the stultifying uniformity of rural Ireland in the 1950s as attention-seeking. But Seán, who was naturally inclined to those who were a bit out of the ordinary, grew up determined to plough his own furrow.

Seán spent two years in Rockwell and proved to be a diligent student. But by 1940, his mother was becoming increasingly frail and was finding it difficult to manage without him. Besides, the school fees were a considerable drain on her financial resources. It was a sign of the high regard in which Seán was held in Rockwell that the college authorities pleaded with his mother to let him attend the school for another year and offered a significant reduction in the fees. Canon Cloney was also anxious to see Seán complete a further year's schooling and wrote a cheque to pay for the bulk of the much-reduced fees. Ellen relented and Seán returned to Rockwell for one more year.

That August, shortly before Seán left for school, the war in Europe came closer to the Hook. Seán was at home at Dungulph when he heard a loud explosion. He rushed to the top of the castle and then heard another explosion. From the top of the castle he could see a large column of black smoke to the north and a plane going up into the clouds. A German plane had dive-bombed the Shelburne co-op in Campile, which his father had helped found. Three women who had been sitting in the co-op canteen were killed. Seán and his uncle later visited the scene of the bombing and attended the funerals of the victims.

Seán left Rockwell for good in 1941. Two years later, his mother died at the age of fifty-seven. Seán was just sixteen and now solely responsible for running the 116-acre farm. His uncle was one of his main sources of support. That same year, Fr Sylvester Byrne became the new curate in Poulfur. In the Diocese of Ferns, a particular system of 'half parishes' had evolved since the Great Famine because of a decision taken by the bishop at that time that every community that had a church should have its own priest. In the rest of Ireland, a curate would report directly to his parish priest, who would report directly to the bishop. But in the Diocese of Ferns, a curate reported directly to the bishop and held control of his 'half' or curacy of the parish. In those days, the curate in Poulfur was the priest who tended to the needs of Fethard's Catholics and was on a par with the parish priest who lived in the parish house in Templetown.

Shortly after arriving, Fr Byrne decided to build a new school in Poulfur and hit upon the idea of staging a play in Fethard to raise funds. The curate took it upon himself to manage all aspects of the production from sets to casting. Byrne chose *The Able Dealer* by J. Bernard MacCarthy for his first production. Byrne selected a cousin of Seán Cloney's for the lead role. But when he was forced to withdraw from the play following the death of a relative, Seán was drafted in as his replacement. The curate believed that his previous acting experience and his schooling best qualified him for the role despite his young age. The first hurdle to overcome in staging the play was finding a suitable venue. Fr Byrne settled on a building, called the 'coal yard', owned by a Catholic publican. The 'coal yard' had only a clay floor and a galvanised iron roof, so members of the Poulfur Dramatic Class, as they were known, had to construct a stage using timber planks laid out on iron tar barrels. Jute sacks were sewn together to create a primitive curtain. With no heating in the building, the actors shivered their way through rehearsals during the cold winter months. Their efforts paid off: the play was a great success, generating much-needed income for the parish, and other productions followed. Four years later the parish had enough funds to pay for its share of the construction of the new school.

Though the labours involved in adapting the 'coal yard' to stage these parish productions no doubt helped the creative imagination and fostered a spirit of camaraderie, there already existed a ready-made venue in the village. The Church of Ireland national school at the back of one of the houses in the middle of Fethard's main street also served as the Protestant parish hall. It was large enough to accommodate a badminton court and had a substantial stage.

The number of Protestants living in Fethard in the 1950s was small – about fifty attended St Mogue's on Sundays – but numerous enough that Catholics on the Hook nicknamed the village 'Little Belfast'. In the sphere of work, the Catholics and Protestants of Fethard interacted easily enough; good neighbourliness and good business sense prevailed. But in the social sphere, things were different. Most Catholics and Protestants became anxious when their offspring kept company with a member of the opposite sex from the other side, fearing that they might get notions of walking to the altar.

In the 1950s, if the Catholic bishops were not denouncing a Communist plot, they were denouncing a Protestant one. In fact, they were often interchangeable, as far as certain members of the hierarchy were concerned. Catholic schoolchildren pitied the poor Protestants who were going to hell for their beliefs. It was forbidden to go into a Protestant church, so that in 1949, during the state funeral of the first President of Ireland, Douglas Hyde, there was the spectacle of government ministers loitering outside St Patrick's Cathedral like a bunch of shuffling alcoholics outside the pub waiting for opening time. On the other hand, the aloofness of some Protestants, especially the older generation of church elders, understandably riled many Catholics, who identified their behaviour with the subservience their parents and grandparents had often been expected to display towards their 'betters' during the landlord era.

Relations between the Catholic clergy and the Church of Ireland rector in Fethard were 'very formal', Seán Cloney recalled. 'There was a feeling or belief abroad that Protestants were heretics and should be converted from the error of their ways, if possible.'[6] This 'very formal' relationship soured with the arrival of a new rector in Fethard in 1942. Reverend Rutherford was an Englishman who had formerly been Rector of Timahoe in County Laois. The rumour around Fethard was that he had got himself appointed to an Irish parish so that his son would not have to serve in the war. Whatever his reasons for coming to Ireland, Rutherford soon realised that the Church of Ireland was not in a healthy state.

The Church of Ireland had experienced decline since the foundation of the State. Finding a partner of the same religion in rural parishes in the Republic was difficult. Many Protestants ended up marrying Catholics. The children of these mixed marriages would, with few exceptions, be brought up as Catholics, as stipulated by the 1907 *Ne Temere* papal decree. Protestants marrying Catholics had to sign a solemn pledge that they would raise their children as Catholics. In a bid to reverse this decline, Rev. Rutherford set up a social club in the parish hall to give young Protestants an opportunity to meet suitable marriage partners. It proved successful. According to Seán Cloney: 'Within months of his arrival in Fethard, there was a new resurgence in his congregation's sense of identity. In fact its vision of its own importance in the wider community was greatly enhanced.' But this new self-confidence in the Protestant community came at a price. Rev. Rutherford barred Catholics from attending the social club for the reason that it would defeat the purpose of renewing the Protestant congregation. As Cloney noted:

> From his point of view and that of many in his flock that was a quite sensible position to adopt, but, unfortunately, it did not appear in quite the same light to the surrounding Catholic majority. They saw this cleric as a bigoted Englishman, cowardly running away from his own country to save his son's skin and coming to their village where he was making a very serious effort to divide people because of religious allegiances. The admission or non-admission to the fun and games in Fethard School created a 'them and us' situation and while it was there already, it was now re-emphasised afresh.[7]

The arrival of a new Protestant rector in 1946 and of a new Catholic curate in 1947 seemed to mark the beginning of warmer relations between Catholics and Protestants in the village. Rev. Edward Grant was rector for ten years in Fethard. When he left the village in 1956, he thought that 'friendly relationships had developed between me and the 2

Dungulph Castle as it looked at the time of the boycott.

George Bassett, William Hornick and Michael Cloney (l–r). It was well known in Fethard that Michael Cloney, a Catholic and brother of the parish priest, was good friends with the Protestants Bassett and Hornick c. 1920.

Seán Cloney with his father, Michael, c. 1931.

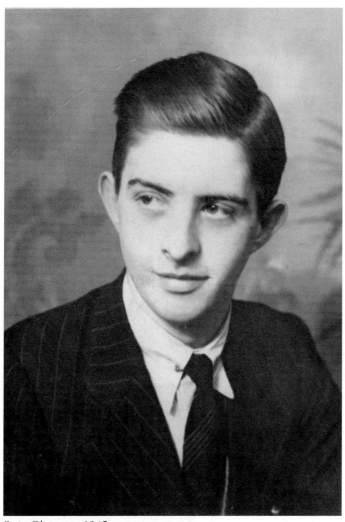

Seán Cloney c. 1945

Seán Cloney on holiday with Sheila in Folkestone in the south of England in October 1948, shortly after they started going out together.

Seán and Sheila Cloney in Trafalgar Square in London on their wedding day, 8 October 1949.

Sheila Cloney's parents, Tommy and Mary Kelly, at John's Hill c. 1955.

Tommy Kelly with one of his prize bulls c. 1955.

Fethard-on-Sea as it looked about the time of the boycott. The house with the car in front of it on the left-hand side of the street housed the Church of Ireland Fethard School. Betty Cooper's shop was three doors down from the school. Leslie Gardiner's shop was on the right-hand side of the street in the tall building farthest from the camera.

Seán Cloney's uncle, Canon Thomas Cloney, who was parish priest of Templetown from 1911 to 1955.

Eileen and Mary Cloney at Dungulph Castle in a photograph taken in 1957, which appeared in many of the newspapers during the boycott.

RC priests and their people'.[8] There certainly seemed to have been a more active engagement between the two religious communities. Rev. Grant and Fr William Stafford, the new Catholic curate, would organise badminton matches between the Catholics and the Protestants in the Protestant school, an indication that Grant took a more sensitive approach to inter-church relations than his English predecessor.

Fr Stafford was from Kilmore Quay, the fishing port on the south Wexford coast where day-trippers and bird watchers embark for the Saltee Islands. He had worked as a priest in the northeast of England before arriving in Fethard, first among the miners at Penshaw in Durham and later in Newcastle.

Fethard was a quiet farming and fishing village in the 1950s. There were a few pubs, shops, a post office, the Protestant national school and a Garda barracks. The fifteenth-century Fethard Castle and the venerable St Mogue's Church, framed by its tidy little graveyard, where the local Protestants attended Sunday service, marked the village's medieval centre. There was no Catholic school or church in Fethard. The modern village had been laid out by the Protestant landlord in the eighteenth century and did not provide for the educational or religious needs of the Catholic tenants. The nearest Catholic church was St Aidan's in Poulfur, a mile and a half to the north of the village and only a stone's throw from Dungulph. Most villagers attended Poulfur rather than the more distant parish church at Templetown, a couple of miles south of Fethard on the road to Hook Head, where Canon Cloney said Mass. St Aidan's is older than the parish church at

Templetown. Dating from before Catholic Emancipation in 1829, the church is hidden in a hollow in the bend of the road leading out of Fethard. Poulfur harks back to a time when Catholic worship was furtive and displeasing to the eyes of the Protestant landlord. It was built on the site of a Mass rock and Mass house, its location dictated by the Loftus family, who insisted that it should be hidden away in a hollow.

There were two Protestant-owned shops in Fethard in the 1950s: Leslie Gardiner's shop sold hardware, groceries, drapery and seeds; Betty Cooper, a local woman in her early twenties, ran a newsagents and sweet shop. Gardiner was born in County Cavan but had grown up in Belfast where his father, an RIC sergeant, had moved the family. It was in Belfast that he first got involved with the Co-operative Movement. He came to Wexford when he got a job in the co-op in Campile. In the 1940s, he moved to Fethard to open his business. Betty Cooper's shop was on the opposite side of the street. There was also a shop run by the wife of the principal of the Catholic national school in Poulfur.

Fr Stafford was a man in a hurry and worked hard to improve the material and social lives of his parishioners. The Hook, like the rest of the country, was stricken by high unemployment and emigration and during his fifteen years in the parish Stafford was to the fore in helping his parishioners to try to find work, though often without success in the stagnant 1950s. Stafford was also centrally involved in trying to persuade people to welcome the benefits of the Electricity Supply Board. In order for an area to be connected to the electricity supply, all the householders had to agree to its installation. But elderly people often were fearful about the cost or the dangers of electricity. It was Fr Stafford who would gently chat to them, gradually winning them over to the advantages of 'the electric'. Stafford was not a tall man but he exuded presence. He was boisterous, enthusiastic and energetic. He was gregarious, good company and fond of a chat and a joke among friends. Many women found him attractive and he seemed to enjoy the company of women. A great GAA man, he was an enthusiastic supporter of the local football club, St Mogue's. But there were aspects to Fr Stafford's character that manifested themselves in more negative ways. He was inflexible, temperamental and unwilling to see other points of view.

Three years after his arrival in the parish, Stafford was involved in a disagreement with Canon Cloney. The row was over the curate's idea of converting the 'coal yard', where the Poulfur Dramatic Class staged its plays, into a proper parish hall. Many Irish towns and villages had no communal meeting place outside of the pub. The pub, in the days before the arrival of the lounge bar, was a male-only environment. The construction of parish halls gave local people somewhere to come together away from the 'social evils' occasioned by the consumption of strong drink. Rural organisations such as the Irish Countrywomen's Association and the young farmers' organisation, Macra na Feirme, were dependent on having a meeting place in the village. The parish hall had the added benefit from the Catholic clergy's point of view of being under their control. Nothing immoral – such as the staging of a dance or an unsuitable play – could take place under the beady eye of the priest. The hall was also another handy way of raising revenue for the parish coffers. Despite Stafford's conviction that a parish hall was crucial to the social life of the village, his parish priest, Canon Cloney, would not sanction the plan. The elderly Cloney argued that the parish already had considerable debts from the construction of the new school at Poulfur. But Stafford was determined to press ahead. Seán Cloney witnessed the aftermath of one heated discussion between his uncle and Stafford. An angry Stafford stormed out of the room after their meeting. Canon Cloney was similarly exasperated and asked his nephew pointedly, 'Do you know that man?'

Frustrated by his parish priest, Stafford paid a visit to the Bishop of Ferns, James Staunton, to get permission. The bishop sanctioned the plan.[9] St Mary's Parish Hall, once built, was a huge success. Plays continued to be staged there, as well as whist drives and fund-raisers for the GAA. It was one of Stafford's lasting achievements. But it was also to become the cause of more bitter disputes in the village.

5

Seán and Sheila

Seán Cloney and Sheila Kelly grew up within a mile of each other. Sheila's father, Tommy, was the Protestant farmer and dealer who had bought the cattle off Seán's mother during the desperate days of the 1930s. Young Seán and Sheila both attended the local Catholic national school at Poulfur. Tommy Kelly had moved Sheila from the Protestant school in Fethard because he thought she would receive a better education at Poulfur.

In July 1948, Seán travelled to Bury St Edmunds in Suffolk to tie up the affairs of a deceased relative. On his way back through London, he called on Sheila, who had followed one of her sisters to England after leaving school and was now working as a domestic servant for a Jewish family in Golders Green. They started going out together when Sheila returned to Fethard for a visit the following month.

The Fethard-on-Sea Boycott

The couple realised at an early stage that their relationship was going to cause problems at home. The Cloneys were part of the south Wexford Catholic establishment. Canon Cloney was a renowned cleric and many of Seán's other relatives were priests. Seán himself had been at one time marked out as a possible candidate for the priesthood. Fr Stafford instantly disapproved of Seán's relationship with Sheila and banned him from taking part in the local drama group. He told Seán that he did not feel his continued presence in the Poulfur Dramatic Class was advisable now that he was going out with a Protestant.

Over the next twelve months, Seán and Sheila travelled back and forth across the Irish Sea. In October 1948, they spent a weekend in Folkestone in Kent. A pair of holiday snaps taken during the trip show a smartly dressed couple clearly enjoying the anonymity and freedom of a few days stolen away from prying eyes. Sheila beams at the camera in one photograph. In the other, Seán poses theatrically, cutting a roguish figure in his three-piece suit complete with slicked-back hair and Clark Gable moustache. The following Easter, Sheila returned to Fethard – seemingly for good. But because of the continuing disapproval of their relationship at home, it seems that just a few months later Seán and Sheila were possibly considering emigration.[1] On 1 August 1949, they both returned to England where they stayed in Bury St Edmunds. On 8 October, they took the plunge and were married in a registry office in Hendon – a picture taken on their wedding day shows them posing in Trafalgar Square. Their decision to get married in a registry office is interesting. It suggests that Seán agreed with Sheila that their marriage would be based on mutual respect, an acknowledgment of each other's religious viewpoints.

Seán and Sheila were renting a post office box in Dublin so they could write to their families back at home – an indication that they did not want the clergy back in Fethard to know where they were staying. But somehow a priest got hold of their address and arrived on their doorstep in Bury St Edmunds. The next month, after some coaxing, Sheila agreed to get married in a Catholic church. On 27 November 1949, a Saturday night, the couple were married in a Catholic ceremony in the Augustinian priory in Hammersmith by the Prior, James Larkin, who was originally from Gusserane, close to Fethard. Since Sheila felt this was one-sided, a blessing in an Anglican church was also arranged. The couple decided to stay in London initially, returning only briefly for the funeral of Seán's uncle, Garrett. An example of the unease felt by the couple was that Seán decided to return to England on Christmas Eve to 'avoid public Church attendance'.[2] But despite help from good neighbours, who looked after the farm while he was away, Seán knew he had to get back to Dungulph. In the summer of 1950, the couple spent a week on holiday in Paris. Both Seán and Sheila had wanted to see the city and realised that once they returned to Wexford they might never have the opportunity again. On the plane home, Sheila fainted. It turned out she was pregnant. Seán and Sheila returned to Wexford in August 1950. The following April, Sheila gave birth to a daughter, Eileen. Two years later, Mary was born.

Hubert Butler, the Kilkenny writer who spent time in Fethard in 1957, portrayed the young Cloney family in his contemporary essay 'Boycott Village':

The Fethard-on-Sea Boycott

Seán Cloney, in his press photographs, looks a pleasant, good-looking, easy-going young man. He has that amused, cynical, shoulder-shrugging appearance that is common enough in Ireland. Sheila Cloney, who has hitherto escaped the press photographer, seems to have been more vigorous and dominating. Immediately after her marriage she started to make the 116-acre farm at Dungulph pay, wrestling herself with the tractor and the accounts and achieving such success that last year they bought a combine harvester. She was as devoted to her own Church as to her home and, when she came in from the fields, as often went with broom and scrubbing brush to the Protestant church of Fethard. It was being redecorated this spring and she was among the most tireless of the volunteers, who every night tidied away the builders' débris.[3]

Sheila was indeed a strong-willed woman who was determined that her children would be brought up in both religious traditions. She had been raised in a 'regular churchgoing farming household'[4] in a dwindling Protestant community. She had a strong faith and was anxious that her children would be conscious of the Protestant tradition from which they came. The couple attended their own churches – Sheila going to St Mogue's in Fethard, Seán going to Mass in Poulfur – and there was a broad understanding that the children would be brought up in both religious traditions. But despite Sheila's determination to raise her children, at least partly, in the Protestant tradition, both Eileen and Mary had been baptised as Catholics, as prescribed by the *Ne Temere* papal decree.

Seán and Sheila

Pope Pius X had issued the *Ne Temere* decree in 1907. It came into effect the following year. The decree regulated the canon law on marriages. It allowed for priests to carry out marriages between a Catholic and a non-Catholic subject to the non-Catholic giving certain guarantees – usually in written form – that any children would be baptised and raised as Catholics. Sheila had agreed to bring up any children from her marriage as Catholics prior to the Catholic marriage ceremony and signed a document to that effect.

According to Rev. Grant, the Church of Ireland rector in Fethard during the decade up to 1956, the Cloneys had intended to baptise Eileen in the Church of Ireland first, and then have a second baptism in the Catholic Church. The reason for this was that the Catholic clergy did not recognise Church of Ireland baptisms as valid, whereas the Church of Ireland *did* recognise baptisms carried out by a Catholic priest. But the nuns in the Catholic nursing home where Eileen was born had had her baptised immediately, removing the possibility of her also being baptised in the Church of Ireland. The same thing happened following the birth of Mary. Grant believed that 'this was an infringement of the couple's policy of mutual regard and joint planning' and 'something which Sheila, a forthright character, would not forget'.[5] Sheila made sure that her third daughter, Hazel, who was born in 1961, was baptised in the Church of Ireland.

While Sheila Cloney was anxious that her husband would not have a monopoly on deciding the religious upbringing of her children, she had already promised, under pressure from the Catholic priest who married her to Seán, to raise them as Catholics by signing the *Ne Temere* pledge. In the eyes of the Catholic Church, she had agreed to bring the children up exclusively as Catholics. Any protestations from the couple that they had agreed to raise the children in both faiths would be met by the argument that Sheila had promised to bring up the children as Catholics and that they had been baptised as such.

A few months after Sheila signed the written pledge to bring up her children as Catholics following her church wedding in London, the Tilson case came before the High Court in Dublin. Ernest Tilson was a Protestant who had married a Catholic in a Catholic church in 1941. In 1950, after differences with his wife, he had put his eldest children into a Protestant children's home and stated that he wanted them brought up as Protestants. Their mother, Mary, applied to the High Court for their return. Before the *Ne Temere* decree had come into effect, it had been traditional for boys to be raised in the same religion as their father and girls in the same as their mother. However, under the common law, the father was the head of the family and had the right to decide in what religion his children would be raised. But in his ruling in the Tilson case, Judge George Gavan Duffy stated that the constitution allowed such precedents to be overthrown. Gavan Duffy ruled that the 'ante-nuptial agreement upon religion is treated under the law of Ireland as a weighty factor in a contest between parents as to their children's creed'. Given that these written agreements were designed to make sure children of mixed marriages were raised as Catholics, this was an explicit recognition of *Ne Temere* in civil law. Gavan Duffy went further:

> In my opinion, an order of the court designed to secure the fulfilment of an agreement, peremptorily required

before a 'mixed marriage' by the Church whose special position in Ireland is officially recognised as the guardian of the faith of the Catholic spouse, cannot be withheld on any ground of public policy by the very State which pays that homage to that Church.[6]

Gavan Duffy ordered that the boys be returned to their mother. The case went on appeal to the Supreme Court. The Supreme Court stated that there was no need to bring into the argument Article 44.1.2 of the Constitution, recognising the special position of the Catholic Church, but upheld the decision by a majority of four to one. They argued on the basis of Article 42 of the Constitution, which stated that it was the duty of the parents, importantly, in the plural, to provide for the education of the children, that having made a decision to raise the children as Catholics, it was not in the power of the father or the mother to revoke it. The one dissenting voice was the Protestant member of the court, Judge William Black, who wondered would the court have found in favour of the mother if she had been the non-Catholic in the marriage.[7]

The judgment was an endorsement by the State of *Ne Temere* despite the fact that the Supreme Court had ruled on the basis of Article 42 of the Constitution which acknowledged 'the primary and natural educator of the child is the Family and guarantees to respect the inalienable right and duty of parents to provide, according to their means, for the religious and moral, intellectual, physical and social education of their children'.[8]

In Fethard, the Catholic priests were determined that the Cloney children would attend the Catholic school at

Poulfur. Seán was also inclined towards sending them to Poulfur. Despite his wife's attitude, he would have preferred to have seen them raised as Catholics. But Sheila saw things differently. As far as she was concerned, the understanding she had with her husband to bring up the children in both traditions was being undermined. The approach of Eileen Cloney's sixth birthday increased the tension in the Cloney household. Eileen was now at compulsory school-going age, and Seán and Sheila had put off a decision about where she should be educated. Seán was coming under increasing pressure from the Catholic clergy in the parish to make sure his daughter was sent to the school at Poulfur.

Seán's uncle, Canon Cloney, had died two years previously at the age of ninety-one. The Canon's replacement as parish priest was Fr Laurence Allen. A native of Gorey in the north of County Wexford, Allen was from a staunchly nationalist family. His brother, Denis, was a Fianna Fáil deputy who had first been elected to the Dáil in 1927. The Allen family had continuously held a seat in Wexford for over half a century. When Denis died in 1961, his 21-year-old son, Lorcan, contested the seat and became the youngest candidate to win a seat in the Dáil. Laurence was active in the Gaelic League and the Feis Ceoil during his time as a curate in Wexford town. In 1933, he was transferred to Boolavogue, where he stayed for twenty-two years, helping build the memorial hall, dedicated to Fr Murphy of 1798 fame, and the new school. Shortly after he arrived in Templetown, he founded a branch of the Legion of Mary. Fr Stafford had been in the parish for more than a decade by the time of Fr Allen's arrival, and found in his new parish priest a more pliant superior than the stubborn Canon Cloney.

Seán and Sheila

Unemployment and emigration were ravaging the Irish countryside in the 1950s. Young men and women, unable to find work, were leaving the country in their droves. By 1957, this was having a perceptible effect on the schools in Fethard. Both the Protestant Fethard School and the Catholic Poulfur School were under pressure because of declining numbers. Poulfur was in danger of losing one of its three teachers, while Fethard School was close to shutting down altogether. Both the Catholic and Protestant clergy, as managers of the schools, were anxious to keep up numbers. The Cloneys found themselves caught in the middle. The Catholic priests were putting pressure on Seán Cloney to send Eileen to Poulfur. On the other hand, Sheila was becoming more anxious and unhappy about the idea of sending her children to the Catholic school.

At the beginning of 1957, Sheila was 'increasingly determined that the children should attend the C[hurch] of I[reland] National School in Fethard – if they were to go to school at all – and Seán seemed to agree with her', according to Rev. Grant. She was taking her stand in the context of a succession of disappointments as regards the couple's 'policy of mutual regard and joint planning'.[9] Her efforts to raise her children partly in her own culture had come to naught and she was faced with a situation whereby her children would be educated in an ethos that was openly hostile to her own Church.

Seán knew that Sheila felt betrayed and he may have agreed at some point with his wife that the children should go to the Protestant national school in Fethard. But he also had divided loyalties: between his wife and his undertaking that the children would be raised in both faiths and a natural preference that they attend the Catholic school. Otherwise, why did it take so long to come to a decision about Eileen's schooling? Fr Allen and Fr Stafford reminded him of his duties as head of the household and as a good Catholic. They told him to stand up to his wife.

Unwisely, Fr Allen decided to force the issue during a visit to Dungulph Castle in the spring of 1957. Forty years later, Seán Cloney recounted what occurred:

> I was out working on the farm one day and the local parish priest came on a visit to my wife. The object of the visit was which school was Eileen going to go to. We hadn't discussed it seriously and it hadn't been resolved. He pre-empted that. Before he left he said: 'Eileen's going to the local Catholic school and there's nothing you can do about it'. Sheila didn't fancy being ordered. She developed the frame of mind, 'we'll see what could be done about it'.[10]

Allen's visit was not an isolated event. According to Rev. Grant, Dungulph Castle was being 'more and more frequently visited by the two locally concerned Catholic Priests' as Eileen approached her sixth birthday. In April, Sheila received a visit from three Catholic priests: Fr Allen, Fr Stafford and the priest who had officiated at the Cloney's marriage ceremony in London, James Larkin. Unsurprisingly, Sheila Cloney felt the presence of three Catholic priests in her home intimidating. The clergy had already interfered in her life when they had cross-examined her doctor about the possibility that she had given birth to a previous child.[11] Fr Stafford later argued that the visit to

Seán and Sheila

Dungulph Castle by the clergy had been a friendly one, contrary to a statement he said Sheila had made.

On several occasions Sheila told Seán she didn't want the children 'to be brought up as Catholics' and threatened to go away to 'think things over'. By late April, her attitude was hardening. On 15 April, Sheila asked Seán for money. He went to see her father and told him that she was thinking of leaving. On 20 April Sheila told her father that she was planning to leave Fethard with the children. He gave her £30 for a short trip. Three days later she raised a further £32 by selling a litter of pigs. Seán believed that 'her father and family did their best to stop her from leaving'.

In 1997, Seán recalled the day Sheila finally left. It was a Saturday. He had gone out to work in the fields at about 9 a.m. 'On April 27th, I knew she was on the point of leaving, but it was not up to me to restrain her. When I came in at lunchtime she was gone, the children were gone, the car was gone. I visited her parents and her brother and told the guards. Word came from the guards that the car had been abandoned in Wexford town. I had no idea where she had gone.'[12]

Sheila's journey got off to a bad start. She hit one of the gateposts as she manoeuvred the family car out of the entrance to the farm, an omen of the difficult days ahead.[13]

6

News from the North

The crowd waited for the show to start. They were packed into Belfast's large Ulster Hall on a December night in 1956 to see a fiery young preacher and a teenage schoolgirl. The preacher's name was Ian Paisley, the thirty-year-old founder and moderator of the fundamentalist evangelical Free Presbyterian Church of Ulster. The girl's name was Maura Lyons. Maura was a fifteen-year-old Catholic from West Belfast. That autumn, while working as a stitcher in the Star Clothing Company on the Donegall Road, Maura had attended a Pentecostalist prayer meeting and experienced a revelation. On the advice of a fellow worker, she met the minister of the local Free Presbyterian church. He later introduced her to Paisley, who invited her to his wedding. On 18 October 1956 she became a Free Presbyterian. Her family reacted angrily to her decision. Her father beat her, priests were called to the house to pray with her and it was decided that she should be sent to a convent. But five days later, with her bag packed and three priests waiting downstairs, she slipped away through her bedroom window and sought help from the Free Presbyterians. Paisley's deputy, John Wylie, smuggled Maura out of Northern Ireland to England and then on to Scotland. The newspapers picked up the story that November. It became front-page news on both sides of the border. Paisley denied that he knew Maura's whereabouts, but the following month posters went up all over Belfast suggesting that Maura would be present at an event presided over by Paisley at the Ulster Hall on 20 December.

Paisley was then still relatively unknown. His tiny Free Presbyterian Church was made up of only a handful of congregations. But his anti-Catholic rhetoric and criticism of the errors of mainstream Protestantism was slowly beginning to attract a following. He was already adept at spotting good opportunities for publicity. His narrative for Maura Lyons was a poor Catholic girl who had renounced her Romish superstitions and been 'born again', only to have a gang of tyrannical priests try to force her into a convent – the type of story that played to the anti-Catholicism of prejudiced Northern Protestants.

Thousands flocked to the Ulster Hall to catch a glimpse of the benighted girl who, as Paisley would have it, had been rescued from the clutches of the nuns. Paisley finally appeared at the top of the hall to a rapturous reception. But there was no sign of Maura. Beside him sitting on a table was a tape recorder. As the hall settled down, he pressed play. A disembodied voice began: 'My Roman Catholic religion had been fear and dread. The new religion to which

I was introduced was simple and free from fear.' It was Maura relating her terrible experience at the hands of the Catholic Church. The girl herself was still across the Irish Sea in hiding. But it did not matter. The crowd lapped it up.

Despite an extensive search by the RUC, by the police in Britain and by the Garda Síochána, Maura remained in hiding until May 1957 when she turned up at the manse beside the Ravenhill Free Presbyterian Church in Belfast, home to Paisley and his wife. Paisley – who had, as usual, plausible deniability of how she had ended up in front of his house – brought Maura to the RUC where she was reunited with her parents. The meeting was not a happy one. Maura was terrified that she was still going to be locked up in a convent and did not wish to go home. Her father assaulted Paisley's solicitor, wrongly assuming he was one of his daughter's abductors. Maura was made a ward of court. When the case later came before the Belfast High Court in May, the Lord Chief Justice made her father guardian but warned him that there should be 'no interference by the family, friends or neighbours with the girl's religious freedom'.[1] Maura later renounced her conversion and returned to the faith of her family, but not before Paisley and his followers had carried off a significant propaganda coup. It was followed by two less high profile conversions – that of Kathleen Kelly, an eighteen-year-old from a Church of Ireland family who also worked at the Star Clothing Company, and that of Denis McCann, an eighteen-year-old Catholic from Portadown.

Two weeks before Maura Lyons reappeared in Belfast, Sheila Cloney arrived in Northern Ireland with Eileen and Mary. Her idea was to seek help from the Church of Ireland.

News from the North

Sheila may have found echoes of her own situation in the Maura Lyons case, which had received wide coverage south of the border, and believed the best place to find a sympathetic ear was among northern Protestants. Sheila and the children had driven to Wexford from where they were taken to County Monaghan. The rumour in Fethard later spread that Sheila's brother, Tom, had driven them to the border. Sheila and the children spent their first night away from home in the Charlemont Arms in Armagh. The following night they stayed in a Salvation Army hostel in Belfast. For the next three nights they were in a boarding house on the Ravenhill Road in Belfast.

Rev. George Thompson, the head of the Irish Church Mission in Belfast, took Sheila and her children under his wing. Thompson was an associate of an East Belfast Baptist called Norman Porter, a member of the Northern Ireland parliament at Stormont and a political ally of Paisley. Porter and Paisley had first met through their membership of the National Union of Protestants (NUP), an English-based evangelical association set up to lobby against High Church tendencies in the Church of England. In the late 1940s Paisley and Porter travelled to London to seek permission – successfully – to set up an Irish version of the NUP. The Irish NUP was a very different animal from its English cousin. Paisley and Porter's NUP was determined to defend Northern Ireland as a Protestant state for a Protestant people and condemned Catholic efforts to buy land and property in an effort 'to establish the Papacy in Ulster'. The NUP provided a platform for the young Paisley to hone his anti-Catholic rhetoric and denounce the government in the South.

The Fethard-on-Sea Boycott

It was through Porter that Paisley met Desmond Boal, a young barrister from the working-class Fountain area of Derry. Educated at Trinity College in Dublin, where he had founded an Orange lodge, the politically ambitious Boal was a keen and original political thinker. In 1960 he won a Unionist seat at Stormont. Despite his party membership, he was deeply antagonistic to the Unionist establishment and was to become one of the most vociferous critics of Prime Minister Terence O'Neill's attempts to improve relations with the Republic's government later that decade. Boal's political career was to become intertwined with that of Ian Paisley. They developed a long-standing friendship and in 1971 broke the mould of Unionist politics in Northern Ireland by founding the Democratic Unionist Party (DUP). In 1957, this network of ambitious hardliners recognised an opportunity to repeat the success of the Maura Lyons case in the plight of Sheila Cloney and her children.

Three days after Sheila's disappearance, Boal drove into the yard at Dungulph and trudged across the fields to introduce himself to Seán Cloney. Over a cup of tea in the castle, Boal told Seán he had met Sheila in Belfast and that he had come to deliver what he described as her terms of settlement. According to Seán, these were:

> That I should sell my property in County Wexford.
> That I should go to Canada or Australia with my wife and children.
> That I would agree to the children being brought up in the Protestant faith.
> That I would consider changing my own religion.[2]

Both Seán and Sheila Cloney were later insistent that she had known nothing of the demands. Sheila was particularly scornful of the idea that she would have considered asking her husband to change his religion. 'It wouldn't have even entered my head, let alone to suggest it,' she said later.[3] 'Those demands did not come from her – she did not formulate them – she knew nothing about them until she saw me eight months later,' said Seán Cloney.[4]

But at this stage Seán believed that his wife would not meet him unless he agreed to the terms beforehand. Boal advised him to make up his mind quickly about the proposal because Sheila was going to a secret location that would not be disclosed to him. The barrister added that he was meeting Sheila the next day and hoped to remain in contact with her for the next two weeks. Cloney told Boal that he did not agree with his terms. At about 8 p.m., after three and a half hours of discussion, Boal got into his car and drove back to Belfast.[5]

Seán Cloney immediately sought the advice of Fr Allen and Fr Stafford. They told him to recover the children, and that the parish would pick up any costs incurred. Cloney then consulted a local solicitor and the next day travelled to Belfast. There he consulted another solicitor, James Doran, who went to the RUC barracks on Musgrave Street and reported the disappearance of the two children.

On 2 May, Cloney visited Boal at home and demanded to see his wife. He told the barrister that he wanted to talk to her about the question of emigrating. Boal told him that he would be able to get in touch with his wife immediately but not until Cloney had agreed to the terms outlined during their meeting in Fethard. Boal drove Cloney back to his hotel and promised to return in half an hour with Sheila. He did not return. After a meeting with Doran, Cloney called at Boal's house but there was no answer. Cloney called on the barrister again the following day. According to Cloney, Boal accused him of 'not being honest' and closing the door on a settlement with Sheila. Boal told Cloney that he did not know where his wife was but that he was waiting for her to contact him by letter.

Later that day, Cloney's legal team applied for a writ of habeas corpus in the Belfast High Court. After giving details of his marriage, Cloney, in a sworn affidavit read out to the court by his counsel, Ambrose McGonigal, said he and his wife had agreed that any children from their marriage should be brought up as Catholics. 'Eileen should have started school on April 29, but my wife was opposed to her being educated as a Catholic,' the affidavit continued. 'I believe Mr Boal knows where my wife and children are, and that he and my wife are detaining my children and preventing me from seeing them or obtaining custody or control of them.' The writ was granted conditionally against Sheila Cloney because the court did not know of her whereabouts.[6]

While in Belfast, Cloney kept watch at the docks at night, alongside members of the RUC, to see if he could spot his family getting on to one of the boats. He also hired a private detective. But it was to no avail. Like Maura Lyons six months previously, Sheila and the girls had already been smuggled out of Northern Ireland – the day after Seán arrived – this time back across the border to Dublin and then across the Irish Sea to Liverpool. On 4 May 1957, they arrived in Edinburgh where they had been given the name of a Baptist minister, Albert Long, who was the head of the city mission. Long found Sheila a job and lodgings and Eileen finally started going to school. Later, Sheila and the children moved again, this time to the Orkney Islands. But for the moment, she was able to stop running. Little did she know the consequences her actions were to have back in Fethard.

7

The Boycott Begins

The Church of Ireland Bishop of Ossory, Ferns and Leighlin, John Percy Phair, instituted Adrian Fisher as the Rector of the Fethard Union of Parishes in the recently renovated St Mogue's Church on 9 May 1957. Fisher's last post had been as a chaplain with the British Army in Cyprus. During the ceremony, Phair hubristically referred to 'this chaplain, coming from troubled Cyprus, to this quiet outpost of the Church of Ireland'.[1] Though English-born, Fisher had grown up in Ireland, the son of an English father, a former rector of Newbridge in County Kildare, and an Anglo-Irish mother, one of the Burtons of Burton Hall in County Carlow. Fisher was ordained in 1949. For the next three years, the self-described 'pale-faced young curate' served his apprenticeship in Carlow town and Killeshin in County Laois, before rejoining the British Army in 1952. He had previously joined the Irish Guards while in Trinity College. Fisher was stationed with the army in the

The Boycott Begins

Mediterranean when he received a letter from his mother enclosing a note from Lord Templemore, one of the local churchwardens in the Fethard Union of Parishes and a scion of the Chichester family of Dunbrody Park, inviting him to take up the position of rector.[2]

Afterwards, while disrobing in the vestry, the new rector overheard a whispered conversation between the archdeacon and the bishop; the archdeacon was warning Phair of the likelihood of trouble arising from Sheila Cloney's disappearance.[3] After the ceremony, the parishioners gathered for refreshments in Fethard school. During the course of an informal speech, the bishop pointed out how numbers at the school were declining and that the school was in danger of closing.[4]

Two days later, an account of Seán Cloney's court case in Belfast containing details of the couple's domestic dispute was published in the local newspaper. The next day, a Sunday, Fr Stafford said Mass in the church at Poulfur. Most of those gathered in the church knew that something dramatic was about to happen. During the homily Stafford let fly. He denounced Sheila Cloney for taking the children away from their father and their home and accused her of robbing them of their faith. He also denounced local Protestants for having financially aided Sheila Cloney's departure. The curate announced that it was up to the Catholics of Fethard to exert pressure on the missing woman and her co-religionists to make sure the children were restored to their father and that this would be achieved by withholding custom from Protestant businesses in the village. Jimmy Kennedy, a confidant of Fr Stafford, had advised the curate not to use the word 'boycott'. But there was no doubt that was what it was.

The Catholic clergy's justification of the boycott was always that local Protestants had aided Sheila Cloney's departure from the village with financial assistance. It is true that her father gave her money, though he did try to persuade her not to leave. But the allegation of other Protestants financially assisting her seems to have been based on a false assumption. Witnesses had seen Leslie Gardiner collecting money from Protestants in his shop. It was assumed by those behind the boycott that the money was for Sheila Cloney. In fact, the collection had been for the clergyman who had been filling in at St Mogue's in the absence of an incumbent rector. Gardiner visited Belfast shortly afterwards for a family funeral, which added to suspicions.

The Mass-goers had to pass St Mogue's on their way back into the village. Many of them bowed their heads and refused to pass the time of the day with their bemused Protestant neighbours who were chatting outside the church after their morning service.[5] But this was only the beginning. The next day, Monday, the majority of the Catholics in the village and surrounding area obediently began to observe the boycott. They stopped going into the two Protestant shops in the village.

On Wednesday, the Church of Ireland school, attended by eleven pupils, was forced to close after the 22-year-old Catholic teacher, Anna Walsh, resigned. According to a report in *The Irish Times*, a number of women in the village had told her that it 'would be better for her if she did not give any more lessons'. Fr Stafford had advised Walsh the previous Saturday to carry on teaching. Yet by Tuesday the pressure on her to resign had become too much. That afternoon, she informed the parents of the children that the school would not open the next day. The reason she gave to the Department of Education for resigning was 'a boycott in the area'. Mary Stafford, a 63-year-old Catholic, also resigned her position as sexton of St Mogue's that same week. *The Irish Times* later reported that she had been pressurised into doing so by her neighbours.[6] She denied this. 'I knew,' she said, 'the boycott was on and, as a Catholic, my convictions urged me to resign.' She had held the position for seven years.[7] Minnie Orange, a Protestant who had served as sexton previously, was reappointed. Lucy Knipe, an elderly Protestant music teacher living alone in Fethard, also lost her dozen Catholic pupils.

The boycott hit local farmers, too. Sheila's father, Tommy Kelly, found that his neighbours would not deal with him. Catholic labourers told Protestant farmers in the area that they would no longer be able to work for them.[8] Catholics who bought milk from Protestant farmers cancelled their orders.

The Protestants in the village were stunned by the boycott. Unfortunately, their new rector was in Dublin. Fisher was commuting to Fethard from his parents' house in Monkstown while the Georgian rectory in the village was being refurbished and he was ill-equipped for the crisis facing his parishioners. Instead, they turned to his predecessor, Edward Grant, who had been the incumbent for over a decade when he left Fethard in November 1956 and who had become well acquainted with members of both religious communities.[9] He knew the Cloney and Kelly families and was aware of the background to Seán and Sheila's domestic dispute.[10] Grant was living in Castlebridge just north of

The Fethard-on-Sea Boycott

Wexford town. On the third day of the boycott, 15 May, Leslie Gardiner and Shelagh Auld arrived at the clergyman's house with news of the school's closure and pleaded for help. Grant was anxious to act from 'a fond, if not a foolish urge to get things in Fethard back to normal' but was conscious of the delicacy of the situation in the village. He was further hindered by the fact that the Church of Ireland General Synod was taking place that week and most of 'the "reliable" and "sound" clergy and laymen' to whom he would normally turn for advice were away.

Grant used his position as secretary of the diocesan board of education to intervene on the issue of the school's closure. After unsuccessfully trying to reach Fisher to inform him of the boycott, he decided to involve Bishop Phair 'as soon as possible, after checking out details which would enable me to make out a report to him'. Grant also decided to deal directly with those whom he believed were responsible for the boycott: the Bishop of Ferns, James Staunton, and the Catholic clergy, Frs Allen and Stafford. He also decided to call on Anna Walsh, the Catholic teacher who had closed the Church of Ireland national school.[11]

Grant called on Bishop Staunton at about 1.30 p.m that same day. He found that the bishop was 'already fully aware of the boycott'. Staunton assured Grant that he had not instigated the boycott but rather that it was 'a "spontaneous" reaction by the people to Mrs Cloney's taking the children away'. Sheila Cloney had left on Saturday 27 April. The boycott had begun two weeks later. Grant wondered about the anomaly of a 'spontaneous reaction' that took two weeks to develop and about how far 'the local priests encouraged, or controlled the people's reaction, and if they would, or could, ease matters'. Grant speculated that the timing of the boycott was directly linked to the celebrations that greeted the arrival of the new rector. 'Was it mere coincidence,' he wrote later, 'that, on the following Sunday, 12 May, just 2 weeks after Sheila's disappearance, the boycott was called from the altars of the 2 catholic churches? – and glee left Protestant faces.'

After his meeting with Staunton, Grant met Allen and Stafford together in Fethard. Allen had refused to be interviewed alone. Stafford did the talking, while Allen occasionally instructed him not to say too much. Grant suspected that the elderly Allen, who used a hearing aid, 'missed much of what Stafford and I had to say' but 'he did "chip in" on one occasion, giving the impression then of thinking, and wanting me to think that he was making a vital point'. Grant recalled: 'From the outset I indicated that I did not approve of Stafford's action. The interview took place in an empty room of a house which, with its contents, was in the process of being auctioned. The atmosphere was not one of "fellowship", and there was an unexpectedly waspish, and a stubborn, element in Stafford's attitude to me.'[12]

This contrasted with Grant's description of their good working relationship prior to the boycott when he had been rector in Fethard. Stafford echoed his bishop's defence of the boycott as 'a spontaneous reaction' by the local Catholics to the taking away of 'their' children. According to Grant, the Catholic curate told him the boycott had been adopted before anything was said in the two parish churches, that it had been 'fired' by a 'conviction that a certain group of the Protestants had encouraged, co-operated in, and financed

The Fethard-on-Sea Boycott

Mrs Cloney's "spiriting away" of the children'.

> When I stated that mention of such a group was a 'bolt out of the blue' to me, I was told I could find out for myself as quickly as 'they' had done. Stafford said that the names of the guilty were known, and that some, who pleaded ignorance, had admitted their guilt as soon as the 'squeeze' came on.
>
> Stafford also said that the Boycott was the culmination of a 'feeling' aroused against the Protestants 2 years previously. I, personally, had never sensed anything of such a feeling during my last year and a half in Fethard.
>
> I could recall only 1st: an objection by Miss Colclough, the Protestant owner of Tintern Abbey, to 'our' holding of a public dance in our Fethard school; and 2nd the 'leaking' of a suggestion, which had been 'voted down', that the Catholic Sexton of our St Mogue's Church should be 'fired' and replaced by a Protestant.[13]

Grant's account of this meeting suggests that resentments over the attitude of the former rector and certain church elders towards Catholic participation in the social and economic life of the church contributed to the hardening of Catholic attitudes towards Protestants in Fethard in the years before the boycott. Though minor, these perceived or real slights, especially when perpetrated by the more elitist elements of the Protestant community – including the remnants of the landlord class, such as the Colcloughs – would have tended to rankle. This was hardly surprising given that the Land War was still within living memory. Inter-church relations were marked mostly by good neighbourliness, as was required in any small rural community. But in the realm of social activity, Catholics and Protestants tended to stick to their own. Catholic cultural and sporting activity revolved around clerical-sponsored events in the parish hall and the GAA, which held little appeal for Protestants. Moreover, the very existence of the religious minority depended on retaining a sense of otherness, culturally and socially. Grant recalled good-humoured occasions during which Catholics and Protestants came together, including the badminton matches organised by Stafford and himself in the Protestant parish hall. But they were emphasised as much by division – 'a Catholic team and a team from "my lot"' – as by togetherness. It should be pointed out that the 'us and them' mentality existed within both religious communities. The Church of Ireland hierarchy encouraged exclusivity, not least because mixed marriages under the *Ne Temere* decree spelt disaster for the Protestant community in Ireland. Bishop Phair, once he finally intervened in the dispute, was at pains to emphasise the trouble caused by mixed marriages.

Stafford's reference to the visit that three members of the Catholic clergy, including Allen and himself, had paid to Sheila Cloney a week before her departure raises the question of economic motives behind the boycott. Stafford told Grant that no pressure had been exerted on her when she had initially refused to allow her elder child to attend the Catholic national school in Poulfur, 'at a time when the retention of a third teacher was proving difficult'. Both schools were facing declining numbers, putting pressure on the school managers, respectively the parish priest and the rector, to increase enrolment. Phair had sounded a warning about Fethard school just three days before Stafford announced the boycott. According to Grant, the school was in jeopardy once Anna Walsh resigned, given the previous term's critical transport average – a reference to the number of children required in a school for the provision of a free school bus service.

During the meeting with Grant, Fr Stafford was keen to contrast what he saw as the clergy's benign influence with Sheila Cloney's stubborn refusal to fulfil her promise to educate her children as Catholics. He noted that Sheila 'had said that her children would never attend a Catholic Chapel' after her husband had proposed to take Eileen to Mass on Holy Thursday the previous year, 'though she had never objected to the priests, mainly Fr Allen, leaving religious pictures and catechisms for the children'. The clergy had intervened when Sheila had brought the children for private tuition to Lucy Knipe, the elderly music teacher and former Sunday School teacher who lived on the village's main street. Grant noted that Fr Allen had pointed out that the clergy had taken steps 'through her husband' to prevent these private classes from continuing, presumably to show that the priests were not telling Sheila directly what she should do, instead preferring to put pressure on Seán by reminding him of his duties as a good Catholic and head of the family.

Another point Stafford made at the meeting with Grant was that a lot of planning must have gone into enabling Sheila Cloney to leave Fethard on a Saturday morning with 'two soft children' and make contact with a senior counsel

The Boycott Begins

in Belfast by the following morning. This was significant, because in order to justify their actions the boycotters had to prove that Sheila Cloney had received help in leaving Fethard. Stafford also acknowledged that the Catholic teacher in the Church of Ireland school, Anna Walsh, had approached him when she heard that there was to be a boycott, to know what she should do. He had first told her to carry on but, a few days later, told her it 'would be just as well if she stopped teaching'. Stafford finished up by telling Grant that the boycott would be maintained until the two children were returned. He professed sympathy for the innocent Protestants but insisted that it was up to them to compel the 'spiriters away' of the children to bring them back. He added that 'Mother Church was weeping for her children, whose souls were in jeopardy'.

Grant drove straight to Anna Walsh's home in Arthurstown, about eight miles from Fethard, after his meeting with Allen and Stafford. His account of this meeting provides further evidence that there were important economic issues at stake during the boycott. Walsh had previously been lodging with the family of the headmaster of the smaller Catholic national school in Templetown, Charlie Hearne. Hearne's wife was also a teacher in the national school in Poulfur. According to Grant, Walsh said 'she had had to leave that house' two days before the boycott began and that she had received threats that she would be 'pelted' if she walked down the main street in Fethard to the school. Under pressure, she decided to close the school. She had informed Leslie Gardiner, whose shop was directly across the street, of her intention to close the school the next day so that parents could be made aware and so as to avoid the school transport contractor making an idle journey. Grant told her that he needed a note from her for the school inspector and the Department of Education in order to keep the school officially recognised because the term had almost two months still to run. The note attributed the closing of the school to the boycott.[14]

Grant's final visit of the afternoon was to the home of Sheila Cloney's brother, Tom Kelly, and his wife, Isobel. Tom was not at home but Isobel told the clergyman that Sheila's family had urged her not to go a couple of weeks before she left. She added that no 'guilty "finance aiding" party' existed and that Sheila's father had given her money, 'without any thought of helping her to flee', and that she had raised additional money from the sale of some pigs. This was thought to be all the money she had had with her when she left. Grant also learned that there were rumours that 'damage was to be done' to Leslie Gardiner's shop.[15] The testimony of Walsh, Fisher, Grant and Isobel Kelly is compelling evidence that intimidation and threats were widespread.

Con Power, who lived near Loftus Hall, close to Templetown church and to the home of the parish priest, was among those who were put under pressure not to deal with their Protestant neighbours. According to Grant, Power was instructed not to go ahead with a cattle deal with Tommy Kelly. To circumvent this instruction, Power arranged to sell them to another party, a Catholic associate of Kelly in Waterford. This man paid Power by cheque for the cattle. When Fr Allen learned of the transaction, he confronted Power and tore up the cheque. On hearing about what had happened, the Waterford dealer instructed a solicitor to initiate proceedings against Allen, but Stafford eventually persuaded him to 'think otherwise'. Isobel Kelly told Grant that her husband, Tom, and his brother, Billy, had gone to Dublin to take up the matter with a solicitor that very morning.[16]

That evening, Grant telephoned Bishop Phair and Fisher, the absentee rector. The bishop arranged to meet him the following day at the University Club in Dublin. Phair told him to collect Fisher at his parents' home in Monkstown on the way. Grant was irritated at Phair's attitude when they met: 'you may guess my feelings when, later, the Bishop's only comment proved to be "You cannot boycott a community".'[17] Grant obviously believed Phair was not taking the boycott seriously. His attitude was to be mirrored by many within the Church of Ireland who felt that their leaders were being too passive and not doing enough to help the Protestants of Fethard. Fisher, on the other hand, was in an even more difficult situation. He had been rector for less than four days when the boycott began; he did not know his parishioners well and was not living in County Wexford, let alone Fethard. It was no wonder that the local Protestants turned to their former rector whom they had known for more than a decade. Grant was sorry that he had not 'accidentally' run into one of the younger bishops while he was in Dublin because he felt that someone like Gordon Perdue, the Bishop of Cork, Cloyne and Ross, might have 'made more' of his report.[18] But Phair did not share Grant's urgency, and so an opportunity to try to resolve the boycott before it became public and the stakes became higher was lost.

8

War of Words

*T*he *Irish Times* was the first newspaper to reveal the existence of a boycott in Fethard, two weeks after it had started. Their circulation department tipped off the newsdesk when Betty Cooper cancelled her order, giving the reason that there was a boycott in the village. Reporter Cathal O'Shannon was dispatched to cover the story. Unfortunately someone in the office got their Fethards mixed up, bought the wrong train tickets and O'Shannon ended up in Fethard, County Tipperary.[1] He eventually managed to get to the correct Fethard and the first mention of the boycott appeared in the pages of *The Irish Times* on 27 May 1957 under the headline: 'Village boycott of school and shops'.[2] After giving the background to the boycott, O'Shannon reported:

> The Protestants are hurt and surprised at the action of their neighbours, and consider that the action of Mrs Cloney is a domestic affair and none of their business.

None of them know the whereabouts of Mrs Cloney or her children.

One Protestant, the father of two children, made a statement to the police at Duncannon, six miles from Fethard, saying that he was apprehensive for the safety of his relatives and asking for police protection.

A Catholic trader said he believed that if the children were not returned to their father the boycott might spread all over the diocese. There would be no peace until they were returned, he said, even though not all of the villagers had their heart in the boycott, or even believed in it at all.[3]

O'Shannon remembers that 'people clammed up' when he tried to approach them because *The Irish Times* was regarded as the paper of the 'Protestant ascendancy class'.[4] The Catholic hierarchy certainly held a particular grudge over the newspaper's coverage of the Mother-and-Child controversy.[5] In initial reports, such as the one that appeared in the paper on 27 May, Fethard's Catholics gave mixed views about the boycott. But within a week or so, they were toeing the priests' line. On 3 June, *The Irish Times* reported that 'the Roman Catholic population is firmly convinced that local Protestants financed and co-operated in the disappearance of this woman and her two children' and that 'there will be no bitterness or violence shown against the Protestant community – only effective action in the form of a boycott'. By now, Betty Cooper had lost the custom of sweet-buying Catholic children and had seen her Sunday newspaper sales drop from around fifty copies to twenty, these mostly to 'Protestants and passing tourists'.[6]

The Fethard-on-Sea Boycott

The incumbent rector, Adrian Fisher, was now in Fethard and making efforts to end the boycott. On 4 June, he condemned Sheila Cloney's actions in a report in the *Irish Independent*:

> She was under a solemn obligation to have the children brought up in the Roman Catholic faith. She broke that solemn obligation and, without a word of warning, disappeared with the children.
>
> I pray to God that I may be pouring oil on troubled waters when I say that everybody in the Church of Ireland certainly condemns her action in running away with the children and breaking up a home.[7]

Fisher said the boycott 'should cease and that the law should try and get the children back'. He added that it was 'unjust that the Roman Catholic community should interfere in this way with Protestants who have had nothing to do with the matter'. On 5 June, *The Irish Press* carried a story that Fisher was considering making representations to the Taoiseach and the papal nuncio.[8] Two days later, the rector appealed to Bishop Staunton and Fr Allen to call a halt. 'Innocent citizens are being victimized and it is so stupid because it is all over a matter which is no concern of theirs,' he said.[9]

Fisher was in regular contact with a wide range of correspondents throughout the summer, including the outspoken Trinity College academic A. A. Luce, the well-known barrister and columnist Eoin 'the Pope' O'Mahony, and the Dean of Christ Church, E. H. Lewis-Crosby, who sent a cheque for £3 in early June to assist the rector's parishioners. 'I consider you are holding the fort for us all,' he said. 'A defeat at Fethard will be a defeat for the Church in the Republic.'[10]

In early June Fisher decided to call on Fr Stafford to discuss how they could resolve the situation. The two men agreed to meet at the presbytery at Poulfur. Fifty years later, Fisher recalled the meeting vividly. At the time he rather naively pictured Stafford as the innocent young curate he had once been. But Stafford had been in Fethard for a decade by 1957. He had spent a further six years as a curate in two other parishes, as well as a couple of years before that in harsh north-of-England mining communities. Stafford was used to getting his way. The clergyman knocked on the door and was greeted by the imposing figure of Stafford. The priest asked Fisher to sit down at a long table covered in green baize, rather peremptorily according to the Church of Ireland clergyman, and then he smashed his fist down on the table inches in front of the rector's nose. Fisher was stunned.

> He [Stafford] said you are to go to Belfast and see a solicitor and bring back Mrs Cloney's children. I had no idea whether she was in Belfast or in England. I said I have no intention of going to the North of Ireland, to Belfast. My duty is here with my people, my parishioners. I've no intention but thank you for your hospitality and I got up . . . I was really shocked.[11]

Stafford ended the brief discussion by threatening Fisher that the boycott would not end and would get worse unless Sheila Cloney returned with the children. It seemed that efforts were already under way to spread the boycott to other parishes in the diocese.

The boycott in Fethard, meanwhile, was getting worse. Three Catholic workers walked off the farm of Henry Auld, one of the local churchwardens. The men had been in Auld's employment for many years. They said to him they had been told to leave but that they would return when the boycott was over.[12]

Three weeks into the boycott, Alexander Auld, a dairy farmer who lived outside the village, had lost 95 per cent of his milk orders. A Catholic man who had a poor credit history and could get tick only in the Protestant shops was told that he must deal solely with Catholic shopkeepers. Another Catholic woman, caught buying milk from a Protestant, was similarly reprimanded. Leslie Gardiner was one of those hit hardest by the boycott. His son, David, believed that 'the boycott ruined his business'. Many customers never came back, even when the boycott was officially ended. Across the street, the newsagent Betty Cooper lost at least sixty customers. Catholic children stopped buying sweets and their parents no longer passed the time of day with her in the street. 'I've lived in Fethard all my life but I may be forced to leave here,' she told the *Belfast Telegraph*. 'If the boycott keeps going I don't think I'll be able to hold out.'[13] Despite her grim forecast, she was still running the shop in the mid-1990s.

The economic and social consequences of the campaign on the Protestant community in Fethard began to be analysed in the press. One letter writer to *The Irish Times* saw mercenary motives behind the boycott:

Those who are actively keeping it going are the lumpen-Catholics, a type to be found in every religion, and those who hope that there will be Protestant shops and farms sold cheap if they keep the pressure up. Most of the people are boycotting Protestants not because they want to but for fear that they themselves will be boycotted if they don't.[14]

Perhaps the worst effect of the boycott was that Fethard's Protestant children were being deprived of an education. The school had been without a teacher since 15 May. At the end of May, the Church of Ireland Training College advertised the position.[15] On 5 June, Owen Sheehy Skeffington raised the closure of the school in the Seanad, the first mention of the boycott in the Houses of the Oireachtas. After first protesting at the absence of the newly appointed Minister for Education, Jack Lynch, or any other member of the government to explain the situation in Fethard, Sheehy Skeffington said that 'the majority of our people, Protestant and Catholic alike, feel ashamed when this kind of boycott of a school takes place'. He said he was

. . . not concerned with the commercial boycott, although I regard it in this case as equivalent to conviction and sentence without trial.

What concerns me is the matter I have asked leave to raise here; and I hope, even though he be absent, that it concerns the Minister also. It is the simple fact that 11 small children are being deprived – I think I might use the word victimised – in relation to the educational facilities and the opportunities for education afforded to them at a most critical age, and at a most critical time of the year.

Sheehy Skeffington then asked if the children were expected to walk to a distant school and, if they were not, would they be prosecuted under the School Attendance Act (1936). The Catholic clergy in Fethard had attempted to put pressure on Sheila Cloney to send her elder daughter to the Catholic national school by threatening prosecution under this same Act. Sheehy Skeffington wondered if the Department of Education intended to supply transport for the children to enable them to get to another school and whether or not any approach had been made by the minister's 'inspectors or by his officials to any responsible and influential local people who might be capable of ending what appears to be a most unfortunate deadlock in relation to this small school'.

Senator William Bedell Stanford, the Regius Professor of Greek at Trinity College and later Chancellor of the University, also spoke on the issue, reiterating Sheehy Skeffington's plea to the minister and the department to take action. Stanford was a member of the Church of Ireland and the only member of either House of the Oireachtas of that religion to comment on the boycott. In 1944, he had published a pamphlet arguing that members of the Church of Ireland, 'despite efforts by the government to prevent it', were under pressure.[16] Those who sought to undermine the Church of Ireland, he wrote, achieved their aims '. . . by obstructing [Protestant] purchase of sites, houses, land, shops; by preventing Protestants from sharing in the control of public works and charitable organisations; by emphasising their social fewness and loneliness; by arguing that to be a true Irishman one must be a Roman Catholic.'[17]

During Stanford's moderate intervention in the Seanad, he described the Department of Education as 'an admirable example of even-handed justice – I would even say, of generosity – in its treatment of the religious minorities' and he called on the minister and his department to do all in their power

> . . . to meet this emergency. By acting wisely and justly in this matter, they will effectively mitigate the unpleasantness of the whole situation. They will not have to make any pronouncement; they will not have to take up any major stand of policy in the matter; but by quietly coping with the emergency in a fair and generous way, they will implicitly remove much of the unpleasantness. I should like to go further. I hope that the members of this House and that Irish men and women of goodwill through the country will join in discouraging sectarian animosity of this kind.[18]

The Fianna Fáil government's spokesman, Éamon Kissane, dismissed the school closure as a local matter which did not concern the department and said the appointment and retention of a teacher was an issue for the school manager. He added: 'Here was a case of a one-teacher school with 11 pupils where the teacher herself decided to give up teaching. There was nothing the Minister for Education could do about that. He could not go down or get his representative to go down, and compel this teacher to stay in the school.'[19]

The Fethard-on-Sea Boycott

Senators Sheehy Skeffington and Stanford had high-lighted one of the most detrimental consequences of the boycott on the Protestant community of Fethard. The agnostic Sheehy Skeffington, son of the well-known pacifist, Francis Sheehy Skeffington, who had been picked up and summarily executed by a mad British Army captain during the 1916 Rising, was an independent-minded figure and attacked the boycott in the columns of *The Irish Times*. Stanford, on the other hand, was one of the most prominent members of the Church of Ireland to criticise the boycott, albeit in a most reserved manner. Neither Sheehy Skeffington nor Stanford represented the mainstream of public opinion. Both had been elected to the Seanad by the graduates of Trinity College, which was off-limits to Catholics on pain of excommunication. Their worthy protest might have caused the Fianna Fáil government some embar-rassment but was not likely to elicit a response.

There was still no replacement teacher for Fethard School by the middle of June when Liam MacGabhann, a Catholic journalist with the then British-owned *People* newspaper in Wexford and a trained national school teacher, offered his services to Fisher. On 11 June he wrote to the rector, putting himself forward as a temporary replacement, with the following proviso: 'I had better inform you that I am a newspaperman and any of my experiences in life may be the subject of the articles which I write. That would include the experience of teaching in the town of Fethard in the strange circumstances which have overtaken it.'[20]

It would have been interesting to have had MacGabhann's first-hand account of life in the village, but before giving a definite undertaking to take over at the school, the journalist wrote to the Archbishop of Armagh and Primate of All-Ireland, Cardinal John D'Alton, making sure that in taking up the position at the school – teaching secular subjects – he would not be 'infringing on any laws of faith or morals'.[21] The reply from Armagh raised no objections to MacGabhann offering his services at the school but advised him to consult Bishop Staunton.[22] MacGabhann, following the Cardinal's advice, wrote to Staunton on 18 June.[23] The following day the bishop sent his reply. In a terse handwritten note, he said that he had nothing to add to what Cardinal D'Alton had written, before continuing: 'I need only add that, if you had approached the matter without bias and made an effort to find out the facts, there would have been no need to write either to the Cardinal or to me.'[24] This stern rebuke was enough to scare off MacGabhann's employers at the *People*. The journalist rang Fisher to tell him the news.[25] Fisher then wrote to MacGabhann regretting that he could not take up the post in view of the fact that the Department of Education had intimated they had no objection. He told MacGabhann that he had mentioned the matter to his own bishop and added that he had promised him that he would send him Bishop Staunton's reply to the journalist's letter. He continued:

> Yesterday I appointed Mr Norman Ruddock of Carlow as a temporary substitute teacher to Fethard National School, but because of the delay in making this appointment, I would be grateful if you would let me know the reason given by your London paper the *People* for not granting you permission to teach in Fethard.

> Were they influenced by Dr Staunton's letter to you in
> arriving at this decision?[26]

MacGabhann answered that the newspaper had found the
reply of Dr Staunton 'too ambiguous to act on'; their 'final
attitude was that as a British-based newspaper their
motives in Fethard would be misunderstood by the Irish
public'. He told Fisher he regretted that he would have to
abandon the idea.[27]

While the boycott continued to be splashed across the
front pages of the newspapers, Seán Cloney was still trying
to recover his children through the Northern Ireland
courts. On 7 June, he was in Belfast for another hearing.
His legal team was seeking to have enforced the
conditional order of habeas corpus previously granted by
the court. A solicitor, Gwendoline Sullivan, who had been
put in touch with Sheila when she first arrived in Belfast
was ordered by the judge to write down the name of the
house where they had met. Sullivan had previously claimed
privilege but eventually consented to writing it down on a
piece of paper which was then made available to counsel.
Justice Sheil adjourned the case for a week to see if further
evidence of Sheila Cloney's whereabouts could be
produced. During the hearing, the issue of the boycott was
raised in court. Cloney stated that it had nothing whatever
to do with what was taking place in Fethard and said he
regretted it very much.

The Fethard clergy had put considerable pressure on
Cloney from the moment his wife and children disappeared.
During the first weeks, he had relied on the counsel of the
priests and dutifully did what he could to recover his

children. By early June, however, he could see that the boycott was not only unjust – his in-laws were among those who were being hurt the most – but that its effect would be the opposite of what was intended: it was likely to prolong the break-up of the Cloney family. A week later, on 14 June, Seán Cloney was back in the High Court in Belfast to hear the two judges formally refuse to enforce the conditional order for habeas corpus. The case was left open, much to the fury of the boycott ringleaders back in Fethard.

Meanwhile, the boycott had taken a decidedly nasty turn. Reports of shots being fired outside the houses of Protestants around Fethard began to appear in the press. Sheila Cloney's brother, Tom Kelly, sought police protection after being awakened in the middle of the night by shots outside the window of his house in Battlestown, a few miles north of Fethard. Kelly was about to go outside but his pregnant wife, Isobel, stopped him by grabbing on to his legs. She was terrified and a few days later had a miscarriage. In the presence of Fisher, who described the shooting as 'rank intimidation',[28] Tom and his brother Billy Kelly made a statement to the gardaí in which they both stated that they believed there was a danger to themselves, their relations, their lives and their property. The gardaí paid regular visits to both men's houses from that point on.[29]

Norman Ruddock, the Trinity College student from Carlow who had taken over the teaching duties at Fethard School, was also threatened. On the day he began his duties, he walked across the street to the school to find a piece of cardboard pinned to the door with the following words written on it: 'Scabs. Beware of the lead in the boycott village.' The notice was handed in to the gardaí.[30]

Ruddock, despite the hostile environment, tried to make the children's lives as normal as possible, but it was not always easy. He recalled the visit of a school inspector who 'examined the children in a very aggressive manner'. The school was in danger of losing its free transport service because of declining numbers and, according to Ruddock, the school inspector drove from the school to each of the children's homes, checking mileages to ensure that each pupil was the required distance from the school to avail of the service. Ruddock says that when he returned, the inspector 'was in a foul humour and insinuated that the distances were wrong . . . It was like an inquisition. I have always regretted that I did not complain to the Department of Education about the inspector's behaviour. I could see where his sympathy and loyalty lay'.[31]

On 21 June, the lead story of the *Standard*, which had close links to the Knights of Saint Columbanus,[32] was headlined: '"We Have No Boycott" Say These Wounded Catholics'. The article, based on information obtained by a 'special reporter' sent to the village to investigate the 'so-called "boycott",' repeated the boycott leaders' official line.

'We have no boycott here,' the Catholics told him. 'We have acted without direction or leadership of any kind. This protest has not been organised. If there were a boycott, labour would have been withdrawn from the fields; there would have been no social intercourse with the Protestants.

'The fact is that no labour has been withdrawn. Catholics still employ Protestants. Some Catholics still buy in Protestant shops. No pressure has been brought to bear on these Catholics. They are free to do what they please.

'We have been deeply wounded by what has been done. Of our own accord we have acted to show our resentment and disapproval of the wrong that has been done to us. We have every right to do that. We have exercised the unquestionable right of every man to shop wherever he wishes, to refuse to co-operate with those whom we feel have hurt us and still continue to hurt us by their lack of response to our appeals for help to get our children back.'

The Catholics seemed to be speaking with one voice to the *Standard*'s man in Fethard, evidence that the newspaper was publishing the boycott leaders' official line, rather than the view of the ordinary man or woman on the street. The influence of the Knights may be detected in the editorial of the same edition. It noted that, in Fethard, 'although the Protestants number only five per cent of the population, they hold a much greater proportion of the public positions'. The editorial continued:

The villagers felt a natural and burning resentment against what had been done. According to all the available evidence, a handful of them decided, independently and spontaneously, to withdraw their custom from the Protestant shops. In doing so they were exercising a natural right which is not infrequently exercised in Ireland by Protestants – without any provocation.[33]

The Fethard-on-Sea Boycott

The *Standard*'s preoccupation with the exalted economic position of the Protestants in Fethard seemed to support the view of the more vocal Church of Ireland commentators who saw the boycott as an assault on local Protestants as much for reasons of wealth redistribution as for Catholic sentiment.

By the end of June, there had still been no public comment from the Catholic hierarchy about the boycott. An editorial writer in the *Church of Ireland Gazette* believed that the silence of the Roman Catholic authorities could 'be taken to mean only approval'.

9

Vigilantes and Gunmen

At the beginning of 1957, Fr Stafford and Fr Allen
had decided to introduce a new system for collecting parish dues. The two priests visited every
Catholic family in the parish to inform them that a new
envelope system was going to be put in place whereby
households would give their weekly contributions to an
appointed collector for their area. Shortly after the boycott
began, Stafford invited these collectors – numbering about
ten or twelve men – to the parish hall in Fethard. When
they arrived, they were told that their duties would now
include acting as vigilantes to ensure that no one in the
village was breaking the boycott. Every Monday night, the
vigilance committee, which Stafford chaired, would meet
in the parish hall to ensure that Catholics in the village
were complying with the boycott. Self-appointed local
vigilance committees, set up to protect public and private

morals, were common in the 1950s. Often they were closely linked to national Catholic organisations such as the Catholic Truth Society, the Irish Vigilance Association and the Knights of Saint Columbanus.

The most prominent leaders of the boycott were those who had the biggest stake in a successful prosecution of the economic campaign against the Protestant community and from the attendance of the two Cloney children at Poulfur school: the clergy, teachers and shopkeepers. Jimmy Kennedy was a butcher in Fethard and a good friend of Fr Stafford. He was also chairman of Wexford County Council. Kennedy was from a strongly republican family. During the War of Independence, the Black and Tans regularly conducted searches of the family home. Kennedy's father had been a chairman of the local branch of Sinn Féin, while an uncle had served time in jail for his IRA activities. The Kennedys were Fianna Fáil through and through. Jimmy and his brother Martin ran a small country store close to the family home in nearby Sheilbaggan, which sold everything from animal feed to donkeys' shoes. They were fervent GAA men, sharing a passion for football with Fr Stafford. They were also devout Catholics. Both Jimmy and Martin were Pioneers, members of the Total Abstinence Association;1 and despite having a reputation for being fond of women, Jimmy was responsible for setting up a body called the Chastity League, which involved him driving along the road at night policing courting couples behind the hedgerows. Kennedy's roles as politician, businessman, member of the local vigilance committee, Knight and all-round fixer gave him considerable clout.

Vigilantes and Gunmen

From the beginning of the boycott, Fr Stafford and Kennedy would discuss tactics with other prominent Catholics in the village. They included Pat Neville, the headmaster of Poulfur national school and a near neighbour of both the Kellys and the Cloneys, who had scooped up Mary Bob's land from under the nose of Tommy Kelly. Neville's wife, Kitty, earned herself the nickname 'Kitty Boycott' such was her zeal for the cause. The Nevilles had a particular interest in the boycott. Pat Neville was in danger of losing a teacher in the school because of declining numbers. Where young Eileen Cloney went to school could tip the balance between keeping or losing a job. Mrs Neville, meanwhile, ran a shop in the village. During the boycott, the owner of the shop in Poulfur, Dave Breen, would send extra papers to Kitty Neville to provide for the customers Betty Cooper had previously served.

Charlie Hearne was the headmaster of the national school at Templetown. His wife was also a teacher. She taught in Poulfur, but, because of declining numbers, she was in danger of losing her job in 1957. It had been pressure from the Hearnes which had forced Anna Walsh to give up her job at the Church of Ireland national school.

Jim Gleeson, who had been one of the trustees of the land at Fethard Castle, was an acolyte of Fr Stafford. The boycott was his idea, as was using a group of vigilantes to enforce it. He himself used to sit at the top of the main street in Fethard in his car, making sure that no Catholics went into either of the Protestant shops. He also tried to spread the boycott to neighbouring parishes, albeit unsuccessfully.

The handful of local Catholics who were opposed to the boycott in Fethard were mostly former members of the

IRA who had been excommunicated by the Catholic Church during the Civil War. The most prominent among them was John Joe Ryan. Ryan was a businessman and cattle dealer who lived with his housekeeper at the bottom of the main street in Fethard. He did not have much time for priests and had stopped attending Mass. On the day Fr Stafford announced the boycott, Ryan went into Leslie Gardiner's shop and told him what had happened. He also told Gardiner that he would back him to the hilt and would send his housekeeper up to Gardiner's shop to buy supplies.[2] On Monday nights, John Joe Ryan would stand outside the parish hall heckling members of the vigilance committee as 'barren old men' as they arrived to attend Fr Stafford's meetings.[3] On another occasion, Sheila Cloney's brother, Tom Kelly, who was specifically targeted by the more zealous boycotters, was on his way from the seashore to the Kelly family home at John's Hill when his tractor broke down on Fethard's main street. Some local men looked on, without coming to his aid. The elderly Ryan sent a man down to help Kelly start the tractor.[4]

Andy Bailey was another former IRA man who had little time for the boycott. Bailey had a history of arousing the displeasure of local clerics. A former IRA quartermaster, who had spent a decade in the United States after deciding to get out of Ireland during the Civil War, he returned to Wexford in the mid-1930s and bought a property called Dungulph Mills, just up the valley from Poulfur church. Pat O'Brien, the deceased former treasurer of the local IRA, had been the previous owner. Bailey bought the property in the hope of finding IRA funds which he believed O'Brien had hidden in the house. But, despite extensive searches, he found nothing. Instead, he turned to modernising the mill's operation. He bought a tractor – one of the first on the Hook – installed a water turbine to drive the hammer mill to grind animal feed and generate electricity, and turned to rearing pigs. It was this latter activity that brought him into conflict with the local curate.

Bailey was a colourful character and tended to think big, perhaps as a result of his ten years in the United States. In 1940, having built modern piggeries to hold his pigs, he decided to construct a large open-air holding tank for the pig slurry. Unfortunately, the smell wafted down the valley to attack the sensitive nostrils of the then curate in Poulfur, Fr Nicholas Redmond, who was noted for his fastidious habits, one of which was to make a show of placing his handkerchief on the chair he was about to sit on when visiting parishioners. The curate, displeased by the smell of the pigs, enlisted the help of neighbour Jim Gleeson, the Blueshirt who had fallen out with Pat O'Brien during the Treaty split, and who also did not have much time for Bailey. The two men decided to confront Bailey about his pigs. Bailey's response was to increase his pig numbers. But disaster struck that winter when one of the walls of his slurry tank collapsed. The noxious contents passed down the river not twenty yards from Poulfur church and Fr Redmond's home. At this stage Fr Redmond's nerves were shot and the bishop transferred him shortly afterwards. Bailey decided to up sticks as well and moved into Fethard to run a pub. A few years later, still attracted by the economic opportunities of pig flesh, he decided to buy a pile of pigs' heads, advertising them outside his pub in Fethard. But they did not sell and the heads started to rot on the premises. Eventually, after several complaints from his neighbours, the rueful Bailey contaminated another stream when he threw the hundred or so heads over a bridge in the dead of night.[5] During the summer of 1957, Bailey acted as guide to Ted Nealon, then a young reporter covering the boycott for *The Irish Press*. Bailey would begin his day by playing the London stock exchange. He would then show Nealon around the Hook and organised for him to go out on the local fishing boats.[6]

A former local captain in the IRA, Richie Rowe, and his son Johnny, who was married to Sheila Cloney's sister Margaret, also opposed the boycott. Tom Hickey, a cousin of Seán Cloney's – who was married to another sister of Sheila's, Hazel – and two other men, Billy Dillon and Jimmy Molloy, also ignored the boycott.[7] But the majority of Catholics in the village followed orders, many out of fear of the priests more than out of any deep conviction.

10

Knights and Bishops

The Knights of Saint Columbanus had a quasi-mythical aura in 1950s' Ireland. Membership of the secretive lay Catholic order was deemed by the Catholic middle classes to confer certain advantages. This was hardly surprising. At least four members of the first Inter-Party government, which was hit by the Mother-and-Child controversy in the early part of the decade, were Knights: the Tánaiste, Minister for Industry and Commerce and long-serving leader of the Labour Party, William Norton; the Minister for Lands, Joseph Blowick; the Minister for Education and leader of Fine Gael, Richard Mulcahy; and the Minister for Justice, Seán MacEoin.[1] The President, Seán T. O'Kelly, was also a Knight.

The Knights were founded by a Belfast parish priest in 1915 as a lay organisation 'to develop a practical Catholicity among its members, to promote and foster the cause of the Catholic faith and Catholic education'.[2] The early proponents of the Northern-based organisation saw the Knights as spearheading lay Catholic action against the twin evils of 'Orange Ascendancy and British Socialism'.[3] By 1917, the first Dublin council of the Knights was in existence and five years later the order moved its base of operations from Belfast to Dublin. By 1923, the Knights took possession of Ely House in Ely Place – formerly part of the magnificent Georgian mansion owned by the Earl of Ely, Henry Loftus – which became their national headquarters.

Throughout the 1920s, the Knights were linked to the hierarchy's campaign against indecent literature and the evils of the motion picture, the radio, the dance halls and intemperance, and were involved in organisations campaigning against 'evil' literature such as the Vigilance Association and the Catholic Truth Society. Evelyn Bolster, the Knights' official historian, notes that the archives of Ely House contain 'countless efforts made by the Knights to alert Church and State alike to the recurring crises provoked by the media'[4] regarding perceived obscenities. By the latter half of the 1950s, the Knights were in 'virtual control' of the Censorship Board and banning about 600 publications a year. The board banned the work of Ernest Hemingway, Graham Greene, Tennessee Williams, William Faulkner, Dylan Thomas, André Malraux and John Steinbeck, as well as Irish writers such as James Joyce, Samuel Beckett, George Bernard Shaw, Seán O'Casey, Liam O'Flaherty, Sean O'Faolain and Frank O'Connor.[5]

Alongside their work in protecting the public's moral virtue, the Knights' primary objective was to counter what they regarded as discriminatory employment practices against Catholics. As far as the Knights were concerned, much of the business and economic life of the Republic was still disproportionately in the hands of Protestants. Combating 'the anti-Catholic activities of certain commercial firms in the country who excluded Catholics from their employment whenever possible' was among the Knights' main fields of endeavour. In 1943 a resolution was passed that 'we must make a close study of actual conditions, social activities and services where a very determined drive is being made by non-Catholics to take over'. According to Evelyn Bolster: 'Alien, non-cooperating Protestant and other non-Catholic firms were in consequence strenuously boycotted and were deprived of Catholic custom; the argument being that where considerations of social justice were disregarded, financial loss might force these firms to consider their attitude towards their Catholic staff members.'[6]

In some respects the order became a victim of its own success, leaving itself open to the charge of discrimination in favour of its own members. Given the secretive nature of the order and its use of rituals and regalia, it is unsurprising that it came to be regarded as the Catholic counterpart to Freemasonry. In fact, much of the ceremonial the order initially employed, and subsequently ditched, had been borrowed from the American Knights of Columbus, which in turn had copied them from the Freemasons.[7] All the above led to a fraught relationship between the order and the hierarchy. According to Bolster, some bishops '. . . have shown hostility towards the Knights, others have ignored them; others again have merely tolerated them and have invoked them only in times of crisis. All of which would seem to imply that the bishops did not wholly approve of the style or method of lay apostolate pursued by the Knights.'[8]

One exception was the Bishop of Ferns, James Staunton, who had been a member of the order for twenty years and held the order's long-service medal. The Knights were eager to assist the bishops in counteracting Protestant proselytism and were involved in the Catholic Protection and Rescue Society, the aim of which was to counteract the activities of Protestant orphanages, the so-called Birds' Nests, in rescuing unwanted children. The campaign against proselytism was still regarded as one of the 'objects of special work' for the order in the late 1940s. Bishop Staunton told his fellow Knights that proselytism was 'as ancient as the penal laws' but 'its methods had changed'. He further reminded them that 'the proselytisers have the immense advantage of secrecy' and that the 'most potent weapon against the Birds' Nests has been publicity'. He urged the Knights to begin a campaign of publicity highlighting this threat.[9] Staunton believed that lay Catholics were not doing enough to counteract secularism, as embodied by institutions such as *The Irish Times* and Trinity College, which he believed were chipping away at the Catholic Church's position as the sole moral authority on social issues. His outlook was informed by his experience during the Mother-and-Child controversy. Until the late 1940s, Church–State relations had been marked by a lack of discord. The Catholic hierarchy and the politicians shared the same broad outlook. The politicians were happy to let the hierarchy dictate to them on social issues that might infringe upon points of Catholic doctrine, and it was taken for granted that the Church had a special interest in issues pertaining to education and health.

In 1950, Noel Browne, the young Trinity-educated Minister for Health in the first Inter-Party government, which had replaced the long-serving Fianna Fáil government of Éamon de Valera in 1948, proposed a scheme to provide free healthcare to new mothers and children under the age of sixteen. The proposed scheme, which Browne envisaged as being free to all, was opposed by the Catholic hierarchy on the grounds that it was socialised medicine and was contrary to the Church's social teaching. Staunton, then the secretary to the hierarchy, was chosen, along with the Archbishop of Dublin, John Charles McQuaid, and the Bishop of Galway, Michael Browne, to outline the bishops' concerns to the minister. Conflicting accounts from the minister and the bishops emerged later about what occurred at this meeting, but by the spring of the following year, the bishops and the minister were on a collision course. The bishops said they could not support the scheme as it stood, that is, free to all rather than with a means test. Noel Browne refused to back down and amend the scheme, despite the opposition of the hierarchy and his own increasing isolation within the cabinet, many of whom were more sympathetic to the concerns of the Catholic hierarchy and the medical profession than with their ministerial colleague. Without even the support of his own party colleague in the cabinet, the Clann na Poblachta leader Seán MacBride, Browne resigned, but before doing so he secured a promise from the editor of *The Irish Times*, Robert Smyllie, that he would publish the correspondence that had passed between himself, the Taoiseach and the hierarchy.

The Fethard-on-Sea Boycott

It was Browne's decision to leak correspondence to *The Irish Times* that broke the mould. For the first time the nature of the relationship between Church and State was being discussed in public. According the pioneering Church–State historian J. H. Whyte, Browne had thus 'forearmed himself against the possibility that the Irish tradition of not involving the Church in public controversy might inhibit the press from printing the dossier which he had sent them'. Smyllie's promise 'disposed of any hesitation that the other papers might have had' and the correspondence was published in *The Irish Times*, *The Irish Press* and the *Irish Independent* on the morning of 12 April 1951, the day after Browne's resignation as Minister for Health.[10] According to Whyte, 'for a country which was little accustomed to the public discussion of Church–State relations, the flood of information was unprecedented, and it is not surprising that it aroused intense interest'. In an editorial in *The Irish Times* on the same day that the correspondence between Browne, the Taoiseach, John A. Costello, and the bishops was published, the paper questioned why the hierarchy was opposed to the scheme without a means test when a 'Mother and Child scheme embodying a means test is in accordance with Christian social principles'. The editorial added that 'the plain man, unversed in subtleties, will be at a loss to determine why the Church should take sides in the matter at all'.[11]

Nothing had really changed in the relationship between the Catholic Church and the State. Browne himself, in his resignation speech, said: 'I as a Catholic accept unequivocally and unreservedly the views of the hierarchy on this matter.' Browne was more interested in settling scores with his cabinet colleagues who had hung him out to dry. But what he had achieved, unwittingly or not, by going to the newspapers was to lay before the public the nature of the relationship between the bishops and the State. As Costello, remarked: 'All this matter was intended to be private and to be adjusted behind closed doors and was never intended to be the subject of public controversy, as it has been made by the former Minister for Health now, and it would have been dealt with in that way had there been any reasonable person, other than the former Minister for Health, engaged in the negotiations at that time.'[12]

The fallout from the controversy had infuriated Bishop Staunton. In a sermon delivered in July 1951, he compared *The Irish Times*' belief that the hierarchy should not have opposed the Mother-and-Child scheme with the persecution of the Catholic Church under the Communist regimes in Eastern Europe:

> Those who carry on the Cromwellian tradition in our country cannot use these methods, but they have the same aim as their predecessors, the aim which is the Communist aim, to drive the Catholic Church out of the life of this country. Their leading newspaper has told us of this aim, and, considering the forces still at their disposal even here, we should be foolish not to take careful note of it. In our country Cromwellians and Communists can unite in their hatred of the Catholic Church.[13]

By the beginning of the 1950s the Knights had 'moved into happier relations with the hierarchy'. There were sixteen bishop-members of the organisation, including the initially suspicious Archbishop of Dublin, John Charles McQuaid. Bishop Farren of Derry described the Knights as the 'cream of Catholic Ireland', and Bishop Staunton, who had always supported the organisation, went further. He described them as 'a dynamic group, full of initiative' and added:

> Not too long ago there was too much clerical action outside the sanctuary and too little lay. This situation is now reversed and the great interest of the Holy See is Catholic Action of all kinds. In this sphere – while I hesitate to make comparisons – I will say that the Knights are second to none. They are the Commandos.[14]

Staunton was a particular admirer of the Knights' methods, which he said, 'did not proclaim themselves to all and sundry, but which nevertheless conveyed a spirit of quiet, steady enthusiasm' and praised 'a hard core of men, sound and unflinching where Christian principles were concerned'.

The Knights were particularly strong in south Wexford, perhaps owing to the fact that Catholics in that county had been politically organised for longer than other parts of Ireland in order to compete economically with their Protestant neighbours. During the late eighteenth century, disenfranchised Catholic merchants and traders had begun forming an alternative power structure of sodalities and confraternities. This Catholic middle class was nourished on tales of how their ancestors had had their land stolen from them by the hated

Cromwell. James Staunton himself was from across the county border in Kilkenny. He had attended St Kieran's in Kilkenny city and St Patrick's, Maynooth, and taught in both colleges before being made President of St Kieran's. In 1939, he was consecrated Bishop of Ferns in St Aidan's Cathedral in Enniscorthy. Upon arriving to take up residence in Wexford town, the newly consecrated bishop was met by a torchlight procession in which thousands of citizens joined. The bishop was a GAA enthusiast and was, according to the *Irish Catholic Directory*, 'himself a hurler of considerable ability'. His liking for 'native games became even more pronounced when he went to Wexford, and his interest in the fortunes of the Wexford county teams were intense'.[15]

Staunton shared the same cultural outlook as Fr Stafford and Jimmy Kennedy. They were undoubtedly influenced by the long shadow of nationalist history in south Wexford/Kilkenny, which traditionally blamed all Ireland's woes on the Cromwellian, and therefore Protestant, interloper. Certainly in south Wexford, the Knights, to which both Staunton and Kennedy belonged, believed that, over thirty-five years after independence, there remained a job to be done: restoring all economic power to Catholic hands.

The bishop must have known about the disappearance of Sheila Cloney at an early stage. It is even possible that he heard about it on the weekend she left, because on that particular Sunday he was confirming children in Templetown. As to the boycott, it seems unlikely that the clergy in Fethard would have proceeded without some indication that their prelate approved of their actions. Fr Stafford had already managed to win over the bishop on the question of the parish hall, and Bishop Staunton seemed 'fully aware' of the boycott when he met Rev. Grant on 15 May 1957, the Wednesday after Fr Stafford had announced it at Sunday Mass in Poulfur.

Bishop Staunton was squarely behind his clergy in Fethard but baulked at making a public statement on the boycott. Nevertheless, he was active in drumming up support behind the scenes, going so far as to ask for the support of the Supreme Council of the Knights of Saint Columbanus, the order's national decision-making body. A 'long and bitter' discussion took place at the subsequent meeting of the Council in Ely Place in Dublin, which several 'leading local Knights' attended. Vincent Grogan, one of the order's Supreme Officers, attended the meeting:

> I was there as Supreme Advocate and, in the face of a level of vituperation which I have rarely, if ever, experienced, I repudiated the idea of the boycott as downright unchristian (this being taken as an attack on Bishop Staunton, of course) while my brethren of the Executive sat silent. The decision was taken in the end not to support the boycott and the late Prof. C. J. O'Reilly, then Supreme Knight, went down to mollify the Bishop.[16]

Evelyn Bolster says that this was 'apparently one of the situations where the Knights believed there were sufficient protagonists in the field to justify their policy of non-involvement'.[17] But Grogan's account of the meeting seems to suggest otherwise. Grogan went on to become a reforming Supreme Knight who sought to open the workings of the order to the public; and it seems likely that in 1957 he already believed that the Knights should move away from being a furtive, quasi-Masonic body devoted to promoting its members' own interests at the expense of non-Catholics, to a socially responsible and open charitable organisation committed to alleviating the social ills suffered by their less well off co-religionists. His conviction that the boycott was morally unjustifiable may have swayed some members.

Another factor that may have informed the Supreme Council's decision not to support the boycott was its impact in Northern Ireland. The boycott was causing dismay in the Anti-Partition League. One of the main arguments used by the League's activists was 'the contrast between the toleration extended to the religious minority in the Twenty-Six Counties and the constant discrimination practised by the majority against the minority in the Six Counties'. By the beginning of July 1957, the secretary of the League, Tadhg Feehan, was receiving requests from a number of branches for a statement condemning the boycott. Northern members of the Knights would have perhaps been more conscious than their gung-ho Southern counterparts of the damaging implications of the Knights lending their support to the boycott as far as the campaign for equal rights for Catholics in the North was concerned.

On 29 June 1957, thousands gathered along the streets of Wexford's villages and towns to witness Cardinal D'Alton, the Archbishop of Armagh and Primate of All Ireland, travel through the county on his way to the Congress of the Catholic Truth Society (CTS) in Wexford town. The Catholic Truth Society had been founded in 1868 by Herbert Vaughan, a future archbishop of Westminster and cardinal. Vaughan's aim was to produce and distribute cheap pamphlets and tracts for the poor workers in Britain's booming industrial towns and for the first two or three years of its existence, penny books and leaflets were issued for this purpose. Vaughan was one of the great Catholic propagandists in the years following the restoration of the Catholic hierarchy in Britain in 1850. His years editing the Catholic periodical, the *Tablet* – he was also its proprietor – saw him lose readers because of his extreme ultramontanist convictions, and the CTS did not become an immediate success, having lapsed into inactivity after Vaughan's consecration as Bishop of Salford in 1872. It was not until the 1880s that the CTS was re-established. The Catholic Truth Society of Ireland was set up at Maynooth in 1899. According to the *Catholic Encyclopedia*, its purpose was to distribute 'sound Catholic literature in popular form so as to give instruction and edification in a manner most likely to interest and attract the general reader' and 'create a taste for a pure and wholesome literature' which would also 'serve as an antidote against the poison of dangerous or immoral writings'.

The build-up to the CTS congress had been intense. The *People* newspaper had devoted pages to the cardinal's impending visit during the previous weeks; the only competing stories were the New York visit of the All-Ireland winning Wexford hurlers and the local visit of the US Navy destroyer, the USS *Barry*. In Gorey, cheering crowds lined the wide main street to greet the cardinal's arrival, which, at the urging of local politicians, had been lavishly decorated by residents in his honour. In the ancient ecclesiastical capital of Ferns, he was welcomed by the priests of the parish and escorted solemnly to the town boundary. In Enniscorthy, there was a civic welcome and a parade of community groups in uniform, sodalities and Catholic organisations. Bishop Staunton then presided over a Solemn Liturgical Reception in St Aidan's Cathedral.[18] Thousands more turned out to witness Cardinal D'Alton arriving at the Redmond Monument in Wexford town to be accorded a civic reception by the local corporation, a great cheer going up as he alighted from his car. After a procession to the Church of the Immaculate Conception, the Cardinal was honoured with another liturgical reception. At 8 p.m. the Cardinal presided at a public lecture given by a Ferns priest and Professor of Ecclesiastical History at Maynooth, Patrick Corish, entitled 'Modern Techniques and the Propagation of Catholic Truth'. James Browne, the President of St Peter's College, gave the vote of thanks. The following day, 30 June, the cardinal was made a freeman of Wexford town at a ceremony in St Peter's College. With the Pugin-built tower and chapel in the background, the cardinal was presented with a casket containing the decision of Wexford Corporation to confer him with the freedom of the city.

The chairman of Wexford County Council, the pious Jimmy Kennedy, one of the key figures in directing the activities of the boycotters in Fethard, was among the dignitaries in attendance. He welcomed the cardinal with the following words:

> Your most humble and obedient servants the members
> of the Wexford Co. Council welcome you and rejoice

with the people of the diocese of Ferns that you have honoured us by this visit.

We are unanimous that advantage should be taken of this momentous occasion to convey to your Eminence an expression of loyalty and affection for your distinguished person, for the Hierarchy of Ireland and the Supreme Sovereign Pontiff, His Holiness, Pope Pius XII.

Your Eminence comes to us as the distinguished and scholarly successor of prelates reaching back to the days of our glorious patron St Patrick and it is the sincere prayer of the Council that the Divine Providence will spare you long to preside over the destinies of the Holy Church in Ireland.

In this period of danger for Catholic truth, faith and morals, we believe that you have proved and will continue to prove a tower of strength in maintaining the efficacy of the Catholic way of life in Ireland in face of the materialistic and pagan tendencies so marked throughout the world today.[19]

The congress was a triumph for Bishop Staunton, who had organised the event. A full page report on the Cardinal's visit published in the *People* on 6 July was headlined: 'One of the most outstanding religious events in the history of the diocese of Ferns.' But it was the sermon of the Bishop of Galway, Michael Browne, at a Solemn High Mass in Wexford town's Rowe Street Church to mark the closing of the CTS congress on Sunday, 30 June, that drew most attention from the national press. In the presence of Cardinal D'Alton, who was presiding at the Mass, and five other members of the hierarchy on the altar, including the Archbishop of Dublin, John Charles McQuaid, Staunton, and the Bishops of Ossory, Meath and Nara, Browne said:[20]

> There seems to be a concerted campaign to entice or kidnap Catholic children and deprive them of their Faith. Non-Catholics, with one or two honourable exceptions, do not protest against the crime of conspiring to steal the children of a Catholic father, but they try to make political capital when a Catholic people make a peaceful and moderate protest. Do non-Catholics never use this weapon of boycott in the North? Here, in the South, do we never hear of them supporting only their own co-religionists in business and in professions? Those who see the mote in their neighbour's eye, but not the beam in their own are hypocrites and Pharisees.

He continued:

> Here in this Catholic country there are bitter enemies of the Church who are ever watchful for attack and misrepresentation. They are carrying on a constant offensive against the Church in newspapers and assemblies.
>
> They misrepresent the Bishops as being opposed to the Health Act on the ground that it would help the working man. The truth, however, is that the Bishops fear it will do more harm than good to the working man and to the nation.
>
> We have men like Blanshard[21] who attack the

Church venomously. We have non-Catholics in the Oireachtas who lose no opportunity to attack the clergy and the Church.[22]

The first public endorsement of the boycott by a member of the hierarchy had taken place in the heart of Wexford, only thirty minutes by car from Fethard. Six members of the hierarchy were in attendance, including its two most senior figures, the Archbishop of Armagh and the Archbishop of Dublin, as well as most of the diocesan clergy. It was an unequivocal show of support for the boycotters.

That same day, the Bishop of Clonfert, William Philbin, speaking at the Social Studies Congress of the Dublin Institute of Catholic Sociology, said that a concerted effort was being made by Protestants to secure a dominating position in Irish public life:

One had only to read a succession of statements from their spokesmen to see that that was true; offensive statements about the Church were now common form with them.

They claimed that leadership in every community belonged to the minority, and, recalling their long ascendancy in the past, they asserted that they should be the dominant group today.

They recognised that they had positions of influence far out of proportion to their members, yet they were exhorting their members to secure more leadership and power. It was a leadership in thought and ideals that was in question, not mere personal prominence.

Knights and Bishops

I suggest that this is an explicit challenge to a Catholic nation which it would be unwise to overlook. Even if it does not succeed in making us desert our Faith it may do much toward neutralizing our Catholicity, and preventing the application of its principles. It may have done much to this effect already. We may have reached a stage when calling Ireland a Catholic nation will be regarded itself as a challenge and deplored by some Catholics.[23]

Bishop Philbin's remarks were prescient. Despite the grand ceremony, the cheering crowds and the solemn oaths of allegiance from the faithful, the hierarchy realised that no longer could it sit back and expect unquestioning deference. The bishops understood that the Church would have to join battle against the forces of liberalism, ecumenism and secularism, much of it fostered in non-Catholic institutions such as The Irish Times and Trinity College, but also among the more questioning Catholic intelligentsia and artistic community as embodied by Sean O'Faolain's Irish literary periodical The Bell. The bishops had flexed their muscles over Fethard. But just four days later they were dealt a blow from a seemingly unlikely source.

11

'Against all our National Traditions'

On the night of 11 December 1956, the IRA launched the first of a series of attacks on military and economic targets in Northern Ireland. It was the beginning of Operation Harvest or what became known as the Border Campaign, which lasted intermittently until 1962. Probably the most notorious incident of the campaign took place on New Year's Day 1957, when two young IRA volunteers, Seán South and Fergal O'Hanlon, were killed during a raid on an RUC barracks in County Fermanagh. The funeral of the devoutly Catholic South – a former member of the Legion of Mary and the extremist Maria Duce – captured a mood in the country at the time. Thousands lined the streets of Dublin and Limerick to watch his funeral cortège, demonstrating 'just how strong the mystique of self-styled "republicanism" in the 1950s was south of the border'.[1]

'Against all our National Traditions'

The resurgent violence prompted Taoiseach John A. Costello's three-year-old Inter-Party government to introduce internment in a crackdown on the leaders of the IRA. These arrests coupled with the crumbling state of the economy prompted the three Clann na Poblachta deputies in the Dáil, upon whom the government was reliant for its parliamentary majority, to withdraw their support. Costello was forced to call an election in March 1957 which swept Fianna Fáil, with the 74-year-old Éamon de Valera as Taoiseach, back into power with an overall majority.

De Valera's relationship with the Protestant minority was governed by his own sense of religious fair play. That is not to say that he saw the Irish nation as anything other than Catholic and Gaelic, but rather that his own political and religious instincts led him to defend the rights of the religious minorities. Still, this did not mean that de Valera had been averse to playing politics with religion in the past. At the beginning of the 1930s, Fianna Fáil was still trying to prove its credentials as a party fit to govern. Many of its members had, less than a decade before, been condemned by the hierarchy during the Civil War. In 1931, the Cumann na nGaedheal government dissolved Mayo County Council after it refused to confirm the appointment of a Protestant woman, Letitia Dunbar Harrison, as the county librarian. Dunbar Harrison owed her selection to the recently created Local Appointments Commission (LAC). By law, local authorities were obliged to accept the 'recommendations' of the LAC, but when members of Mayo County Council met to give formal approval, they refused to endorse the appointment. Their argument was that Dunbar Harrison's background and education made her unfit to supervise the reading matter of Catholics.

Facing down the council, the government appointed a commissioner to administer the county, and he installed Dunbar Harrison as the new county librarian. However, a boycott of library services then began. Lending libraries across the county returned their books to the central library in Castlebar in protest at Dunbar Harrison's appointment. With the controversy showing no signs of abating and a general election looming, the government offered Dunbar Harrison a post in the Department of Defence's military library in Dublin, which she accepted. The following year, the new Fianna Fáil government restored the functions of the council. During the debate in the Dáil, de Valera, then leader of the Opposition, defended the attitude of the people of Mayo:

> If it is a mere passive position of handing down books that are asked for, then the librarian has no particular duty for which religion should be regarded as a qualification, but if the librarian goes round to the homes of the people trying to interest them in books, sees the children in the schools and asks these children to bring home certain books, or asks what books their parent would like to read; if it is active work of a propagandist education character – and I believe it to be such if it is to be of any value at all and worth the money spent on it – then I say the people of Mayo, in a county where, I think – I forget the figures – over 98 per cent of the population is Catholic, are justified in insisting upon a Catholic librarian.[2]

'Against all our National Traditions'

De Valera may have been influenced by his sympathy for the Catholic people of Mayo or it may have been that 'in the last few years of Cumann na nGaedheal rule, Fianna Fáil was trying to build up an image of being the more truly Catholic party of the two'.[3]

Certainly, once in power, Fianna Fáil under de Valera continued Cumann na nGaedheal's policy of enshrining Catholic moral teaching in the law. The 1937 Constitution embodied de Valera's attitude to the position of religion in the State. Though informed by Catholic social and moral teaching, it bears the unique stamp of de Valera. Divorce was expressly banned, the family was given special recognition and the State's limited rights as regards property and education were acknowledged. Article 44 on religion was cited by critics as evidence of the theocratic nature of mid-twentieth-century Ireland. Article 44.1 began:

1. The State acknowledges that the homage of public worship is due to Almighty God. It shall hold His Name in reverence, and shall respect and honour religion.
2. The State recognises the special position of the Holy Catholic Apostolic and Roman Church as the guardian of the Faith professed by the great majority of the citizens.
3. The State also recognises the Church of Ireland, the Presbyterian Church in Ireland, the Methodist Church in Ireland, the Religious Society of Friends in Ireland, as well as the Jewish Congregations and the other religious denomina-

tions existing in Ireland at the date of the coming into operation of this Constitution.

Article 44.2 continued:

1. Freedom of conscience and the free profession and practice of religion are, subject to public order and morality, guaranteed to every citizen.
2. The State guarantees not to endow any religion.
3. The State shall not impose any disabilities or make any discrimination on the ground of religious profession, belief or status.
4. Legislation providing State aid for schools shall not discriminate between schools under the management of different religious denominations, nor be such as to affect prejudicially the right of any child to attend a school receiving public money without attending religious instruction at that school.
5. Every religious denomination shall have the right to manage its own affairs, own, acquire and administer property, movable and immovable, and maintain institutions for religious or charitable purposes.

The reference to the 'special position' of the Catholic Church, which was removed by amendment after a referendum in 1972, has been the most controversial. Yet, placed in its historical context, the article on religion seems remarkably generous. The explicit recognition of Jewish congregations in a country whose population was overwhelmingly Catholic stands up well in a document drafted in the late 1930s. De Valera's Constitution was framed during a period of intense Catholic sentimentality in the country. The Spanish Civil War was depicted in the Catholic press as an apocalyptic fight between Christian civilisation, as represented by the rebel Nationalists, and atheistic Communism, as represented by the Republic. Rumours of Republican atrocities against nuns and priests and the burning of churches raised the level of the debate to fever pitch. On 16 October 1936, Cardinal MacRory described the Nationalist forces as 'fighting the battle of Christendom against the subversive powers of communism'.[4] But despite calls from Fine Gael to give diplomatic recognition to Franco, de Valera refused to alter the Irish government's policy of non-intervention. De Valera had that trait of Irish Catholics which J. H. Whyte described as 'the ability to profess loyalty to the Church while rejecting its guidance on particular issues'. Early in 1957, that same trait was in evidence in the mourners who flocked to the funerals of Seán South and Fergal O'Hanlon. The hierarchy had formally condemned the IRA in 1956 but that did not stop scenes of extraordinary devotion to the dead gunmen being played out at their funerals.

De Valera enjoyed a good working relationship with the leaders of the Protestant churches. Maurice Dockrell, a Church of Ireland member of the Dáil, who was deputed to visit de Valera to ask him for his help in ending the boycott, remembered that when he first became a TD he was initially prejudiced towards de Valera but later came to respect him as the most practical man in the Dáil. As President, de Valera later appointed Dockrell to the Council of State.[5]

The Fethard-on-Sea Boycott

The boycott hit the news in the wake of a successful high-profile tour of the United States by the Jewish, and Fianna Fáil, Lord Mayor of Dublin, Robert Briscoe. The Republic had been lauded in the USA for its religious toleration compared to the nakedly sectarian government of Northern Ireland. Now Unionists were using the boycott to portray the Republic as priest-ridden and a cold place for Protestants. De Valera was incensed at the damage being done to the national reputation and that a vicious little sectarian dispute was undermining the anti-partition campaign.

De Valera kept himself informed of developments in Fethard through a number of sources. Ted Nealon covered the boycott for the de Valera-controlled *Irish Press*. De Valera 'hated this thing', according to Nealon, and did not want any publicity in the paper. He remembers that much of his copy was spiked. The young journalist was left down in Fethard to keep an eye on things and had to phone the news editor every night in case the Taoiseach rang looking for information. 'The reason I was left down was because they wanted to know what was going on,' he recalled. While frustrated that his reports were not being published in the newspaper, Nealon was filling in journalists from other newspapers, such as Cathal O'Shannon of *The Irish Times*.[6]

The Taoiseach's most valuable source of information was the Minister for Finance, Jim Ryan. Ryan knew the people of Fethard. He was a close friend of the Cloney family, was respected by former members of the IRA in the village and was one of two long-serving Fianna Fáil deputies in Wexford, the other being Dinny Allen, the brother of the parish priest who was promoting the boycott.

'Against all our National Traditions'

De Valera first raised the issue of the boycott at a cabinet meeting on 31 May 1957. He told his ministers that he was considering writing to Bishop Staunton. He also raised the question of communicating with Archbishop McQuaid. At the end of the discussion, the cabinet left it up to de Valera to take 'such action as he might think best'.[7] A draft letter intended for the Bishop of Ferns contained in the Department of the Taoiseach file on the boycott gives an indication of de Valera's sense of outrage:

Dear Lord Bishop,

I am writing you as head of the Government to ask that you use your influence to bring the boycott at Fethard-on-Sea to an end. It is doing harm to us as a nation and as a Catholic Community.

As Your Lordship is, of course, aware, where our people live abroad in U.S., Australia, New Zealand and elsewhere, their proud boast when they are looking for fair play in religious matters, education, etc., is that we here in Ireland behave tolerantly towards the minorities in our midst. To any outside observer, the position in Fethard-on-Sea would appear to be that all the members of a small community are being punished because of the act of an individual over whose conduct they could have no effective control. It is a heartbreak, that, because of the ill considered action of a few, we can be held up before the world to be what we fundamentally are not, as if we were a people who when we have numbers on our side can be tyrannical, cruel and unjust. It is against all

our national traditions, and I ask Your Lordship to
intervene to see that it does not continue.[8]

Cooler heads seem to have prevailed and the letter was not
sent. Four days after the issue first came before the Cabinet,
the Secretary to the Department of the Taoiseach, Maurice
Moynihan, advised de Valera to discuss the matter in person
with the Catholic Archbishop of Dublin, John Charles
McQuaid, before taking any other action. De Valera agreed
to postpone action 'for the present'.[9]

By 14 June, there had still been no public comment
from the Catholic hierarchy. The *Church of Ireland Gazette*
was looking for 'an immediate and unqualified assurance
from the civil power that such persecution of a community
on religious grounds is intolerable and against the spirit of
that Constitution which makes free play with expressions of
tolerance and the determination to cherish the rights of
minorities'.[10] The writer added that 'the law has not yet
been broken at Fethard-on-Sea but to employ such a quibble
as an excuse for inaction would be cowardly in any
government. And no one, so far as we know, has yet had
reason to accuse Mr de Valera of moral cowardice'. The
Gazette believed that the Taoiseach's intervention would
'serve the wider purpose of assuring those citizens of the
Republic who do not happen to be Roman Catholics that
the State is indeed jealous of their democratic rights and
liberties'. This, of course, was exactly what the Catholic
hierarchy did not want.

The next day, de Valera discussed the boycott with
McQuaid, within whose archiepiscopal province Fethard
was located, at the archbishop's house in Drumcondra. The

departmental memo of the meeting written by Moynihan contained the following:

> I understand that his Grace appeared to agree, generally, with the Taoiseach's views as to the inadequate justification, or lack of justification, on the available information for the attitude taken up by members of the Catholic community at Fethard and as to the damaging effect on the national reputation for religious tolerance and fair play which is likely to result from the publicity given to the matter.
>
> The Archbishop expressed a desire that the discussions between the Taoiseach and himself on the matter should be treated as strictly confidential in view of this desire. The Taoiseach instructed me to the effect that any record of the discussion should be kept apart from the official file.[11]

McQuaid had a close relationship with de Valera, initially through their links with Blackrock College. De Valera had attended Blackrock College as a pupil, later taught mathematics at the school and was a frequent visitor all his life (he lived next door). McQuaid, when Dean of Studies at Blackrock, befriended de Valera when his eldest son, Vivion, attended the school. McQuaid was also closely involved in advising de Valera when the latter was drafting the 1937 Constitution.

Crucially, de Valera came away from his meeting satisfied that he was now in a position to intervene in the dispute without McQuaid opposing him. Moynihan's memo indicates a level of sympathy and pragmatism from

McQuaid. On the other hand, McQuaid seems to have been sympathetic to the point of view of his fellow bishops. He enjoyed a close relationship with Staunton. If the latter was to be disappointed at not having more vocal support from his archbishop, there is no evidence that McQuaid reproved his suffragan bishop, and, indeed, his presence on the altar during Browne's sermon in support of the boycott added to the ambiguity. Another factor might have been that McQuaid was mourning his sister, Helen, who had died suddenly the previous month. Her death had deeply affected him.[12]

Prominent members of the Church of Ireland urged the Taoiseach to intervene. They believed that de Valera alone was capable of standing up to the Catholic Church and making sure that tolerance was extended to southern Protestants. On 17 June, the Dean of Christ Church, E. H. Lewis-Crosby, remarked that de Valera had won renown for his fine draft of the Constitution with its provisions for religious tolerance. 'Will he not maintain his renown by speaking words of reconciliation?' A week later, the secretary of the Church of Ireland Diocesan Council of Clogher wrote to de Valera, giving notice of the following resolution that had been passed unanimously at a meeting of the diocesan synod three days earlier: 'That this Synod regards with the gravest concern and distress the boycott at Fethard-on-Sea of the members of our church and unanimously offers its deepest sympathy to the victims of such un-Christian conduct.'[13]

Eminent Catholics were also beginning to protest. Donal Barrington, a barrister and law lecturer in UCD who later served as a Supreme Court judge, speaking at a

Catholic social studies conference, described the boycott as a source of scandal outside the country. He said it was doing damage to the cause of Catholicism and was being interpreted as something that was being done in the name of the Catholic religion. 'We should make it quite clear to our co-religionists that while we have great sympathy with them we consider that what they are doing is an unjust and a terrible thing – the worst thing that happened in this part of the country since the Civil War.'[14]

This was the first public condemnation of the boycott by a Catholic public figure. The *Standard* described Barrington's remarks as 'regrettable' and, referring to the barrister's comparison with the events of the 1920s, commented:

> Well, well, well. How many lives have been taken? How many people have to seek permanent police protection? Are the courts worked to death dealing with breaches of the peace? We remind Mr Barrington that it was inflammatory talk of this kind that drove people along the path of bitterness at the time of the Civil War.[15]

In fact, reports of intimidation taking place in Fethard and local Protestants seeking police protection had appeared in the press since the end of May.

Meanwhile, influential Protestants were continuing to press de Valera. On 2 July, A. A. Luce, the Trinity College Professor of Philosophy, who was playing an active role in trying to bring an end to the boycott, met Rev. Fisher in Fethard. He had met Fisher's predecessor, Edward Grant, two weeks previously. Later that day, he wrote to de Valera outlining the information he had received from the two Protestant clergymen. He told the Taoiseach, 'So far there has been no violence, but there has been the threat of violence.' He added that Sheila Cloney's two brothers had asked for police protection.

> I made particular enquiries as to whether the Protestants of the parish had made a collection to enable Mrs Cloney to go away, or had in any other way connived at her action. The answer is No. Both Mr Grant and Mr Fisher have given me specific assurances on the point.
>
> The situation is getting worse with every week that passes; there is no hope that the affair will blow over, or settle itself. The boycott will go on, unless the voice that called it, ends it.[16]

On 3 July, *The Irish Times* reported the annual address of the Church of Ireland Bishop of Kilmore, C. J. Tyndall, under the headline 'Protestants Are Not Aliens'. Bishop Tyndall, responding to the sermon of the Catholic Bishop of Galway, Michael Browne, the previous Sunday, said, 'There is, of course, no concerted campaign in our Church to kidnap children from their Roman Catholic homes. Surely the bishop must know that such an idea is utterly repugnant.' Bishop Tyndall added:

> I must join issue with the Most Rev. Bishop Browne in his third assertion that the boycott of the local Protestant people is a 'peaceful and moderate protest'.

These people are innocent of any involvement in the affair. The factor is surely of paramount importance. This boycott action has split a friendly, tranquil, little community wide open and it may take a generation to heal up the wounds. Moreover, the issue has become nationwide and even world-wide in its repercussions. To attempt to justify it as a mild little local episode is a bit ludicrous. The bishop's words are badly chosen.[17]

The following day, on 4 July, de Valera wrote a note to Archbishop McQuaid advising him that a question about the boycott was being addressed to him in the Dáil and that, in replying to it, he felt 'bound to express openly the views I have formed on the facts as I know them'. McQuaid thanked de Valera for his courtesy in sending him the reply that 'you feel bound to express on the incident at Fethard-on-Sea'.[18]

Later that day in the Dáil, Noel Browne asked the Taoiseach if he had 'received from, or on behalf of, any residents at Fethard-on-Sea representations respecting the boycott of a section of the population there, and if, in view of the grave and growing disquiet throughout Ireland, he proposed to make a statement on the matter'. The Taoiseach replied:

I have made no public statement because I have clung to the hope that good sense and decent neighbourly feeling would, of themselves, bring this business to an end. I cannot say that I know every fact, but if, as Head of the Government, I must speak, I can only say, from what has appeared in public, that I regard this boycott as ill-conceived, ill-considered and futile for the achievement of the purpose for which it seems to have been intended; that I regard it as unjust and cruel to confound the innocent with the guilty; that I repudiate any suggestion that this boycott is typical of the attitude or conduct of our people; that I am convinced that 90 per cent of them look on this matter as I do; and that I beg of all who have regard for the fair name, good repute and well-being of our nation to use their influence to bring this deplorable affair to a speedy end.

I would like to appeal also to any who might have influence with the absent wife to urge on her to respect her troth and her promise and to return with her children to her husband and her home.[19]

De Valera had unequivocally denounced the boycott and called on the bishops to put an end to it immediately. He had also acknowledged the boycotters' stated grievance that the children had been taken from their home. But, crucially, he had called on Sheila Cloney to 'respect her troth'. There was no mention of Catholic children being kidnapped or the *Ne Temere* pledge.

The Wexford deputy Brendan Corish, a future leader of the Labour Party and a member of the Knights of Saint Columbanus, showed where his sympathies lay when he addressed the Taoiseach. He asked him what steps he had taken 'to find out whether or not there is, in fact, a boycott?' and 'would the Taoiseach endeavour to ensure that certain people will not conspire in this part of the country to kidnap Catholic children?'

'Against all our National Traditions'

Almost fifty years later, during a seminar marking the presentation of the late Corish's papers to the Irish Labour History Museum, Justin Keating, the former Labour Minister for Industry and Commerce in 1973–77, recalled Corish's remarks in the Dáil. During the summer of 1957, Keating was on holiday in New Ross. He and a friend, by way of protest at the boycott, toured the pubs in Fethard teasing the locals. 'We would either buy a Guinness or a Jameson and when we were a little bit into the drink we would start teasing the locals saying "You would boycott a piano teacher but you're drinking that Protestant drink".' Years later when Keating entered the Dáil for the first time as a Labour TD, he told Corish, 'I was in Fethard that summer and what was done was wrong.' He continued, 'He was a little bit taken aback, but then, and I quote this not to damage him but to show his greatness of soul, that's why I am dwelling on that episode, I reiterated, "That was wrong, Brendan" and he hummed a bit and then he said "Yes it was".'[20] Others were less generous. Noel Browne subsequently referred to Corish as the 'Bastard of Fethard'.[21]

12

'Not an Inch'

The Taoiseach's remarks were widely welcomed within the Church of Ireland. The Bishop of Ossory, Ferns and Leighlin, John Percy Phair, described de Valera's statement as 'a very reasonable one' and expressed the hope that 'it would bear fruit'. He later wrote to the Taoiseach thanking him for his statement, which he described as a 'very real encouragement'. Professor Luce visited de Valera the next day. 'There is no doubt at all but he is dead against the boycott and would stop it if he could,' he later wrote to Rev. Fisher. 'I was able to put him wise on a few points, but he really knows all about it and is deeply concerned. It is very hard for him to act: it is up to you not to do anything to make it harder.' Luce urged caution on Fisher:

My friendly advice is
(1) Do nothing provocative
(2) Don't exaggerate the dangers

(3) Be careful what statements you give to the press
(4) Do not try to work up an agitation, unless things get worse
(5) Do what you can to improve good relations locally and respond to any olive branch.[1]

Luce acknowledged that a different strategy might have to be put in place if the situation in Fethard got worse.

Liberal Catholics also applauded de Valera's remarks. Christopher Gore-Grimes wrote to de Valera that 'as a Catholic and an Irishman I have always been proud of the absence of religious bigotry in the South, and I have been deeply grieved by this recent occurrence. Your restrained and eminently Christian statement was of untold comfort to me; and for it I thank you from the bottom of my heart.'[2]

The Taoiseach's comments were also welcome sustenance for both Fethard Catholics and Protestants opposed to the boycott. John Joe Ryan wrote a letter to the Taoiseach five days after his Dáil statement. Ryan said that he could see the boycott was 'unjust' and that it was started by people 'not of our party'. He added that 'no-one wants this thing but an [sic] few who are sending letters to attend meetings'. Ryan told de Valera that the Catholics in the village had 'always got along' with the Protestants and 'found them good neighbours if left to themselves' but that an 'inner ring', with Fr Stafford playing a 'big part', was splitting the Catholics in the village. Ryan wrote that Seán Cloney had told him that 'only for this Boycott he and his wife would have a way out but this thing put an end to it'. He continued: 'Mr T[homas] Kelly, Mrs Cloney's father, is the most charitable man around here and I can swear without doubt has done more for the Catholics than for his own class.' Ryan concluded his letter to de Valera with the cryptic line, 'If I were to give you the full details of this Boycott I would have to go back 80 years'.[3] Ryan was referring to the land agitation on the Hook of the 1880s, and may also have been referring to the purchase of John's Hill outside Fethard by Sheila Cloney's great-grandfather, Robert Hornick, in 1870, which had caused widespread discontent among the Catholics of the village.

On 6 July 1957, two days after de Valera's Dáil statement, Seán Cloney wrote a letter to *The Irish Press*. Cloney prefaced his remarks on the situation in Fethard by saying that 'judging from past experience I know that whatever I say will be very strongly criticised, and as to whether I should say anything at all or not may be questioned to an even greater extent by my neighbours'.

Cloney was opposed to the boycott. It was not an easy decision. He knew he would arouse the hostility of the clergy and many of his neighbours, but he recognised that it was the right thing to do, and that, while the boycott was still in place, there was little chance that Sheila and the children would return. Cloney could see there were ulterior motives behind the boycott. He also knew that members of the Protestant community had not 'connived' or 'plotted' at her disappearance. Indeed, he could see better than most how the boycott was affecting them. Tommy Kelly found that Catholics whom he had counted as his friends were now turning their backs on him. The boycott broke his heart. Cloney was pessimistic in his letter to *The Irish Press* and believed that, despite the Taoiseach's intervention, the boycott could still get worse.

'Not an Inch'

He wrote that '. . . the Catholic Church and the Church of Ireland are now both involved in this unfortunate affair and each day may bring developments which can prove injurious to one or the other or both. No man of any faith provided he is loyal to it, will be happy to see that Church of his embarrassed. In the interest of all should not something be done immediately? Who is prepared to take the first step?' He added that 'should there ever be a post-mortem on this sorry business let every investigator entering this district beware of propagandists without scruple, and gossips without decency or honour'. He continued:

As a husband and a father I have obligations to my family and I am bound to interest myself in their welfare; therefore my chief initial concern is the remaking of a broken home with my wife and children. Can the events in Fethard-on-Sea since early May be shown to have assisted me to attain my goal and what of the future? Can events be expected to follow a different pattern?

Both sides agree that my wife made a mistake by going away with our children. I believe others on both sides have also made mistakes – the rash word and the accusing finger.

It is my belief that we all have a duty to our God and Church, to our country, our family and our fellow-man; in their combined interests I write this letter. Let no one entertain the idea that it has been suggested to me by anyone.

The Fethard-on-Sea Boycott

Cloney ended the letter by asking his fellow-Catholics for their prayers.

> If, as we are told, it could solve the problem of Russian Communism, could it not also solve a much smaller problem here? I, therefore, ask your prayers for my wife in particular – she may be in greatest need of them, for our two children, for our clergy, and let us not forget, in this, their hour of trial, our fellow Christians in Fethard who, like us, also worship God, though it be at a different altar to ours.'[4]

It was a piece of masterful diplomacy. Despite the gravity of the situation, there was nevertheless a hint of Cloney's sense of mischief in his reference to solving the problem of Russian Communism through prayer. Of course, many chose to see it as a betrayal, as the author acknowledged at the beginning of his letter. And his rejection of the boycott was to result in ill-will towards him for a long time afterwards. 'It caused a lot of trouble for me,' he said, forty years later.[5]

Both the Taoiseach and Seán Cloney had denounced the boycott. But there was no softening of position from the local Catholic clergy. The day after the letter was published in *The Irish Press*, Cloney attended Sunday Mass in Poulfur. During his homily, Fr Stafford told his parishioners that

> . . . for some time past, in the newspapers and elsewhere various people have been shouting and screaming at the priests and the people of this parish. The priests of this parish, with a full sense of their responsibility and realising the Catholic issue at stake,

assure the faithful, loyal Catholics of this parish that, in the stand they are taking in defence of Catholic principles, not now, nor in the near future, nor in the distant future, will their priests let them down by asking them to withdraw one inch or to apologise for their actions.

Their priests have the utmost confidence and conviction that the people will persevere unflinchingly, and will not allow anything to happen to mar or besmirch this grand, dignified, noble, loyal, legal profession of their faith.[6]

Cloney walked out. Reporters in attendance asked Cloney about how his rejection of the boycott was affecting his relations with local Catholics. He told *The Irish Press* that, though he was still being received satisfactorily by most Catholics in Fethard-on-Sea, 'some are very cool'. *The Irish Times* reported him as saying that certain local Catholics were 'treating me very differently from the way I was being treated immediately after my wife went away and before the boycott started. They were all sympathetic then.' He added, 'They did not agree with my repudiation of the alleged connivance by the Protestant shopkeepers concerned and my wife's disappearance with two children'. Many of the Catholics in the village were angry that Cloney had broken ranks. They believed that it was up to him to control his wife and if he was not able to do so, he should have stuck with his 'own' people to make sure the boycott was brought to a satisfactory end. But Cloney, after initially going along with the Catholic clergy when his wife had disappeared, had set himself against the boycott, recognising that it was

The Fethard-on-Sea Boycott

Fr Stafford's personal crusade, rather than the 'dignified' and 'spontaneous' protest of the Catholic people against the 'kidnapping' of Catholic children.

Later that evening, after returning home to Dungulph Castle, Cloney sat down to write to the Taoiseach. Firstly, he congratulated him on his Dáil statement three days earlier, noting that he seemed to have had 'access to information which is true and accurate – if only our Catholic Bishops would seek access to the same'.

> You will, I know, share my very grave concern that our Bishops, thereby implying the Church, may make a serious faux pas on this boycott issue. A forced retraction by them sometime in the future would be most embarrassing for us all. At Mass here this morning we heard from the altar the outworn Unionist cry 'Not an inch'; the clergy apparently authorise no relaxation of the boycott, and I doubt if it shall ever cease unless and until they so direct.
>
> Please do not consider me unduly pessimistic but I fear time is running out. The consequence, unless there is a change for the better immediately, may well prove very serious for the Church, the local Fianna Fáil Party, our people in the North and our country as a whole. On the personal side I doubt if a better means than this boycott could be devised to discourage any desire my wife might have to return. I have no idea where she is or the children are.

He added:

'Not an Inch'

> I regret I am unable to give you a general picture of the local reaction to your statement. Naturally the Protestants are pleased and appreciative, in Fianna Fáil, many agree with you completely, others are in a dilemma between 'what the priest says' and 'what Dev says', still others say in effect that your statement was ill-advised.[7]

Indeed, there were many in Fethard who were furious with de Valera's Dáil statement. Jim Gleeson, a Fine Gaeler antipathetic to de Valera in any event, remarked: 'The vagabond, he has put a pitch cap on our clergy.'[8] The local Fianna Fáil cumann was split: some wanted an end to the boycott, while others wished to soldier on.

If de Valera was looking for some relaxation in the stance of the bishops, he was to be disappointed. Bishop Browne issued a statement to the press from his home in Galway that same weekend which pointed out that that it was not against justice or charity to refuse special favours such as one's money or custom to those whom one regards as responsible for or approving of a grave offence. Browne was either ignorant of or chose to ignore the circumstances that pertained in the village. He said he had no reason to doubt that the resentment shown by the people of Fethard-on-Sea was 'moderate in extent and quality'. And he called on Bishop Phair to produce 'a list of names of persons of his flock who are suffering and the nature and the exact particulars of what he calls victimisation'.

> There has been no injury to life, limb or property reported to the gardaí. There has been no picketing of

any Protestant premises and picketing is a recognised and legal method of showing displeasure. The Catholic people have not refused the necessaries of life to anyone, as is involved in the rigid boycott advocated by Parnell.

The bishop repeated his assertion that 'political capital' was being made out of the boycott and said that it was a 'gross misrepresentation' that the events were the result of 'intolerance or hatred for Protestants'. He said that they were due 'solely to justified indignation at a grave wrong', and he concluded by saying that he was

> . . . firmly convinced that the greatest injury to justice and peace is being done by those, whether clerical or lay, who are making political propaganda out of a local incident and are inflaming the passions of those who do not know the facts.
>
> They are trying to light fires of bigotry. They should direct their energy to righting the wrong which has caused this trouble.[9]

In fact, the fires of bigotry were already being built – in the fields of Antrim and Down and the narrow streets of the Shankill Road and East Belfast – just in time for the Orange celebrations on the Twelfth of July.

13

'Outside the Pale'

In 1957, the Church of Ireland's rural population had been in serious decline for over seventy-five years. In 1871, there were 42,000 Church of Ireland farmers in the whole of the island. Forty years later this figure had dropped to under 30,000. The First World War and the birth of the Irish Free State accelerated an already steady decline in the Church of Ireland population. Between 1911 and 1926, its membership south of the border fell from 250,000 to 164,000. By 1946, the last year a census was carried out before the boycott, the southern Church of Ireland population had halved to 125,000, representing just over 4 per cent of the total population. By 1961, this had dropped to 104,000 or just under 3.7 per cent of the total population.[1]

For several decades, southern Protestants in rural Ireland had been suffering a crisis of identity. The ethos of the State was overwhelmingly Catholic and Gaelic: being

The Fethard-on-Sea Boycott

Irish meant playing Gaelic football or hurling on Sundays, having the *cúpla focail*, going to Mass and confession, saying the rosary. So, after independence, Protestants minded their own business.

When the boycott in Fethard began, there were those in the Church of Ireland, such as the elderly Bishop of Ossory, Ferns and Leighlin, John Percy Phair, who believed that the best option was to turn the other cheek. Phair's initial reaction to the boycott was disbelief. When he finally visited the village three weeks after the boycott had begun, he told the twenty-five Protestants gathered in the school to 'be their natural selves, to be kindly and helpful and to go around with smiles on their faces'. Phair also publicly condemned mixed marriages, saying to the press that he did all he could to discourage them. 'I think that people should marry into their own faith and Church,' he said. 'Then these things would not happen.' The bishop also unwisely criticised the publicity the boycott was receiving from the media, saying that if it had not been for the newspapers, it would have faded out.[2] The bishop's passive response to the boycott throughout the summer of 1957 may be charitably put down to the fact that he was then eighty years old and ill-equipped to deal with such a crisis.

Many Southern Protestants wished for a more robust defence of their brethren in Fethard. Morgan Dockrell,[3] a member of the well-known Church of Ireland family who ran a successful hardware business on South Great George's Street in Dublin, was an undergraduate at Trinity College in 1957. In this Protestant 'ghetto', Dockrell remembers feeling 'a certain contempt for the leaders of my faith'.[4] A columnist in the *Church of Ireland Gazette* wrote that it was 'natural enough to dismiss the ill-feeling in Fethard as the outcome of another mixed marriage – the contracting of which is frowned upon by both religious communions, Roman Catholic and Protestant. But for the Church of Ireland Bishop of Ossory, Dr Phair to leave it at that is, we feel, less than justice.'[5]

Others were even more vocal in their criticism of what they saw as the pusillanimous attitude of the Church of Ireland's leaders. Hubert Butler believed that the lack of leadership shown during the boycott mortally wounded the Church of Ireland in the Republic. Butler had fallen foul of the Catholic Church in a celebrated incident five years previously. In 1952, Butler, an expert on the history and politics of the Balkans, had attended a meeting of the International Affairs Association in Dublin with his good friend Owen Sheehy Skeffington. The speaker was Peadar O'Curry, the editor of the fiercely anti-Communist *Standard*, who was to read a paper about the persecution of the Catholic Church in Communist Yugoslavia. At the end of the paper, the chairman of the meeting attempted to end proceedings without taking any questions but he was voted down. Butler, who had himself written extensively about Yugoslavia, got up and attempted to speak about some of the issues O'Curry had raised. One such issue was the forced conversions of members of the Serb Orthodox Church in Croatia by the Catholic Church during the Ustashe regime. At which point the papal nuncio, who unbeknownst to Butler was at the meeting, got up from his seat and walked out. The chairman immediately closed the meeting because of the offence given to the nuncio. The press took up the story and the ensuing controversy saw the Kilkenny-native

Butler condemned by the city corporation and county council. The latter demanded his resignation from its Monuments Committee. Butler was also forced to resign from the Kilkenny Archaeological Society, of which he had been a founder member.

Butler was redecorating his house near Bennettsbridge and would travel the fifty miles to Fethard to buy putty, paint and whatever other supplies he needed from the two boycotted shopkeepers. Under the pseudonym 'Resistance', he wrote two letters to *The Irish Times* suggesting that his fellow Protestants do the same. However, Bishop Phair described the proposed course of action as 'unworthy' and 'senseless retaliation', and advised his people 'not to pay any serious attention to it'.[6] Butler, for his part, believed that Phair handled the boycott 'very weakly' and hoped that he would soon retire. He also criticised Phair as 'very double-faced' for blaming the newspapers for their coverage of the boycott and then complimenting journalists on their reporting.[7]

In a penetrating analysis of what the events in Fethard meant for Southern Protestants entitled 'Boycott Village', first published in January 1958, Butler wrote that '. . . the Church of Ireland is much more than a vast complex of emptying palaces, rectories, cathedrals. In Ireland it is still the spearhead of the Reformation and few people are ready to renounce the liberties won at the Reformation, even when they repudiate the reformers. Father Stafford and his anathemas are as much an anachronism in Ireland as the Anglo-Irish ascendancy.'[8]

Butler was particularly incensed by Phair's condemnation of mixed marriages. He believed this amounted to the

Church of Ireland acquiescing in the Catholic Church's enforcement of the *Ne Temere* decree. In his view, *Ne Temere* was at the core of the matter. When the decree came into force in 1908, Butler noted, the Protestant hierarchy had appealed 'on behalf of the oppressed and helpless to all lovers of justice and liberty to do their utmost by all lawful means for the redressing of a grievous wrong'. Fifty years later the same hierarchy 'made a scapegoat of Mrs Cloney and did not reiterate those protests against *Ne Temere*'. Butler later argued that had the Protestants stood up to the campaign of intimidation in Fethard, they would have managed to cause the abolition of the *Ne Temere* decree. He said 'a great common gesture would have given us courage and confidence and arrested the sad slow Protestant decline. It would have reminded the northern Protestants that we belong together and that they belong to Ireland.' Instead, Butler believed the Protestant hierarchy's attitude bore comparison with Chamberlain's policy of appeasement towards Nazi Germany at Munich in the late 1930s.

Similarly, a Church of Ireland rector in Tyrone expressed himself amazed at Bishop Phair's attitude and said it was the 'plain duty of an alert and impartial press to bring to the attention of its readers an incident of this kind'. He also wondered how buying goods from the boycotted shopkeepers could 'in the name of all truth' be interpreted as 'retaliation'.[9]

The Irish Times and Trinity College Dublin were the two bastions of the Church of Ireland in the Republic. *The Irish Times* actively campaigned for an end to the boycott under the stewardship of its editor, Alec Newman, and was the main forum for debate. In an editorial published four weeks into the boycott, *The Irish Times* condemned the action of the boycotters, describing it as 'the sort of conduct which, while official practice in the nations under Communist yoke, has no place in a 20th-century democracy'. The editorial writer added: 'With the ethics of the *Ne Temere* decree, against which Mrs Cloney is alleged to have offended, we are not concerned at the moment.' In common with Butler and Sheehy Skeffington, the newspaper recognised that the root cause of the boycott was the profoundly unjust *Ne Temere* decree. However, it was felt to be more prudent to attack the injustice of victimising innocent Protestants rather than focusing on *Ne Temere*, which would be widely regarded as a Protestant attack on the social teaching of the Catholic Church.

Professor A. A. Luce was another to make his thoughts known in the letters pages of *The Irish Times*. The Trinity academic had also bought goods from the boycotted shops. He believed that the Protestants in Fethard were being deliberately persecuted for economic reasons. Referring to the outrage in the country over the imprisonment of Cardinal Mindszenty by the communists in Hungary, he concluded a letter to *The Irish Times* with the following: 'Persecution in Hungary and the country's aflame; but putting a few Protestant shopkeepers out of business in Fethard-on-Sea – who cares?' A week later in the same newspaper, Luce saw a more sinister purpose to the boycott than the return of the Cloney children. He believed it was being wielded by local Catholics, supported by their clergy, to force the Protestants out of the area.

This communal boycott has two sides; it is an economic and financial weapon, designed to lessen the output of the farms and put the traders out of business, to close the school and ultimately to close the church. As well, it is a psychological weapon, like those said to have been employed by the Chinese against Christian missionaries. It is felt as a mental torture, especially by lonely, defenceless women. It is designed to make the victims feel that they are outside the pale and do not belong . . .

The Church of Ireland does belong, and is not outside the pale. The Protestants of Southern Ireland, including those of Fethard, have supported law and order from the far-off days of the signing of the Treaty, and have done their duty to the state ever since.[10]

It was a pointed public challenge to the government of an Ireland whose Catholic majority was being constantly reminded at Mass and in their newspapers of the barbarities inflicted on Irish Catholic missionaries by the Chinese communists.

The former rector of Fethard, Edward Grant, echoed Luce's trenchant analysis when he recorded 'a course of action, which I heard later had been proposed by some Catholics. It was, that then [sic] should be finished off, as it were, the "getting rid" of "Prods", which had been somewhat in progress in the early 1920s.'[11] Grant was secretary of the diocesan board of education investigating attendances at Protestant national schools some years later when he first heard that this threat had been made during the boycott. By then, there was not one Church of Ireland school south of a line stretching from Wexford to New Ross, including Fethard.[12]

The *Church of Ireland Gazette* shared this analysis. It declared, after the Catholic bishops came out in support of the boycott, that Protestants in the Republic now knew where they stood: the methods employed at Fethard had the sanction of the Roman Catholic Church, and the boycott was part of a deliberate policy to wield the big stick in the face of the minorities and to 'put them in their place'. The *Gazette* believed it was time for the Church of Ireland's leaders to make themselves heard and wished that

> . . . those non-Roman deputies and senators who do exist suffered less from inaudibility on occasions such as this. There is such a thing as having the courage of one's convictions. Finally, we respectfully submit to our own Archbishops and Bishops that this has ceased to be a local affair. It is tempting to say, in places where relations are of the friendliest, 'it can't happen here'. In the absence of any repudiation of Dr. Browne we must conclude that it can happen anywhere.[13]

The 'inaudibility' of southern Protestant leaders was in contrast to the noise from north of the border. The persecution of innocent Protestants at the behest of the Catholic clergy and hierarchy was political manna from heaven for northern Unionists. One Unionist senator and prominent Orangeman, Joseph Cunningham, proposed an exchange of citizens during a debate in the Stormont parliament. He believed that the Northern Ireland government should extend 'an invitation to come North' and that 'we should offer to exchange citizens, especially these people who are always grousing about the North'. Another Unionist senator suggested that the Northern Ireland government should make representations to the government of the Republic on behalf of the Fethard Protestants.[14]

The boycott was of particular distress to anti-partition campaigners. On 8 July 1957, in a letter to the Secretary to the Department of External Affairs, the Irish Ambassador in London, Con Cremin, wrote: 'The reason, of course, is that the League [The Anti-Partition of Ireland League] has always used, as one of its strongest arguments, the contrast between the toleration extended to the religious minority in the Twenty-Six Counties and the constant discrimination practised by the majority against the minority in the Six Counties. The Fethard boycott naturally tends to undermine this argument.'

One London-based member of the Anti-Partition of Ireland League wrote that 'this intolerant behaviour is a betrayal of all the principles which so many Irishmen, both Catholic and Protestant, died to preserve'. Indeed, the secretary of the League, Tadhg Feehan, received requests from various branches to condemn the boycott.

On 10 July, at their request, Bishop Phair and Senator Stanford visited the President Seán T. O'Kelly in Áras an Uachtaráin to discuss the boycott. By this stage, Phair had shifted up a gear and had called on his Catholic counterpart, Staunton, to use his influence to end the boycott. The following day, a group of prominent Catholics in Northern Ireland issued a statement condemning both the boycott and the IRA's renewed campaign of violence. It described the actions of the boycotters as 'indefensible as the abduction of the Cloney children' and said the 'boycott must be deplored by all right-thinking people of every creed'.

> We have heard with relief that the Government of the Republic of Ireland is taking vigorous steps to co-operate with our Government to suppress the current campaign of terror, to bring those responsible to justice and to restore the rule of law.
>
> We also welcome the statement of Mr de Valera deploring the Fethard boycott and would rejoice to hear of its speedy ending and that the missing children have been found.
>
> Whatever may have happened in Northern Ireland in the past or whatever is to come, we reject organised discrimination, religious or otherwise, because we believe that it is contrary to charity and justice, and therefore, contrary to the teaching of the Church we revere.[15]

One of the signatories, barrister Cyril Nicholson, along with the Nationalist MP Francis Hanna, had met with Cardinal D'Alton two days before the statement was published to make known his worries about the impact of the boycott on the position of Catholics in Northern Ireland. After the meeting, D'Alton wrote to Bishop Staunton advising him of the visit. The cardinal said that he had 'agreed I would drop you a line suggesting that perhaps some competent Catholic layman who knows the facts . . . issue a statement denying there is a general boycott of Protestants in Fethard-on-sea'. He said that the Catholic laymen felt it might 'ease matters here, especially among Protestants of good will (I do not know if there are many of these)'. D'Alton noted that Nicholson and Hanna had been of the view that Fr Stafford's remarks the Sunday after de Valera's intervention in the Dáil would 'not help ease the situation'. But the cardinal emphasised that the return of the Cloney children should be regarded as 'the first and essential act of justice'.[16] Staunton's reply showed he was convinced of the righteousness of the boycotters' actions. 'There is so much evidence of absence of religious bigotry, and absence of interference with Protestants, as to be surprising to anyone who has followed the outcry.'[17]

Meanwhile, the boycott figured prominently in the annual Twelfth of July speeches. The Northern Ireland Prime Minister, Lord Brookeborough, addressing Orangemen in his native Fermanagh, said the events at Fethard were a reminder to the loyalists of Ulster of what could happen if Northern Ireland became part of an all-Ireland Republic. He added that the only safeguard for 'our civil and religious liberty' in Northern Ireland was membership of the United Kingdom. Brookeborough compared the toleration shown by the majority Protestant population of Northern Ireland towards their Catholic neighbours in the face of resurgent IRA violence to the treatment being meted out to Protestants in a tiny village in the Republic. 'Where now is the oft repeated boast of Mr Briscoe, the ex-Lord Mayor of Dublin, during his recent American tour, that minorities in Eire enjoy complete freedom and tolerance? What value have Mr de Valera's proposed safeguards or Mr Costello's guarantees for minorities in a united Ireland in the light of Fethard?"[18]

Brian Faulkner, the Unionist chief whip, warned Northern Ireland's Catholics that the 'recent edicts by their bishops in relation to the beleaguered Protestants in Eire could have serious effects locally'. The Northern Ireland Minister of Education, W. M. May, said the events at Fethard had been deliberately designed to foment trouble and religious bigotry. Stormont MPs repeated the mantra: look what Northern Ireland Protestants could expect if subsumed into a united Ireland dominated by the Catholic Church.[19]

These were bitter words for de Valera and members of the Northern Ireland-based Anti-Partition of Ireland League to stomach. The portrayal of Ireland as a warm place for the religious minorities engendered by Robert Briscoe's much-vaunted tour of the United States paled into insignificance when compared with the negative publicity surrounding the boycott. Nevertheless, a editorial in *The Irish Times* published on 15 July, broadly reflecting the views of southern Protestants, gently pointed out the irony that Unionist politicians were criticising religious intolerance in the Republic:

> The Fethard-on-Sea boycott is undemocratic, unchristian and in every way detestable. At the same time, we confess to some resentment at the manner in which political capital is being made of it in the Six Counties – irresistible though the temptation to Stormont must have been and must continue to be. The history of the Six Counties is not so full of inter-

communal sweetness and light, so conspicuously devoid of sectarian and religious bitterness, that a Northern Minister can fairly make political play with what – so, anyhow, we hope – is the isolated extravagance of a very small part of the Twenty-six-County community.[20]

The *Standard* went further. In an editorial on 19 July, it said world opinion would not be 'capable of such a mistake to confuse Fethard-on-Sea with the Unionist official policy of discrimination, to confuse the momentary absence of a few small village accounts in the books of one or two Protestant businessmen with the total absence of Catholic names, the names of one-third of the population, in page after page of official appointments made by the Stormont regime for the last thirty-five years'.[21] The newspaper further decried Brookeborough's advocacy of Protestant employers boycotting the Catholic workforce. Indeed, it was not just Protestant employers in the North who were condemned for their discriminatory practices. A letter signed 'Anti-Restrictions' and published in the *Standard* reflects the attitude of the Knights of Saint Columbanus to the boycott.

Quite apart from the rights and wrongs of the matter, I feel that the attitude of the people who object to the decision of some member of the Fethard population to transfer their custom from certain shops to others and refer to the resulting situation as a boycott would command much more of our sympathy if we had ever heard of their objecting to the practice of so many of their co-religionists who restrict the staffing of their homes and businesses to the members of the religious minority.

How often do we not see the word 'Protestant' in brackets after such words as 'gardener,', 'typist,' etc. in small prepaid advertisements? I have often wondered why the religion of such people should matter. A few years ago the daughter of Protestant friends of mine obtained a position as typist through an advertisement of this kind and I was surprised to discover that a box number concealed the identity of one of the biggest firms of its kind in Dublin.[22]

One welcome consequence of all this publicity was the flood of cheques that poured into Fethard from all over the world for the relief of the distressed businesses in the village, not least from Northern Ireland's Orange lodges and Unionist associations. The employees of the aircraft-makers Short Brothers in Belfast proved especially receptive to the call for help. They sent a cheque for £154 along with a message of support from the employees who had 'watched with considerable interest your struggle against the vile influence of the Hierarchy of the Roman Catholic Church'.[23] Norman Porter's Evangelical Protestant Society raised £80, which Porter delivered in person to the Protestant shopkeepers in Fethard. The huge response from northern Protestants prompted Bishop Phair to write to the *Belfast Telegraph* at the end of August thanking 'our friends in the North' for their financial assistance. Despite his remarks earlier in the summer about unhelpful publicity in the newspapers, Phair expressed his 'sincere appreciation' to the Northern Irish press, saying that it had been of the

Albert Long, pictured with his wife, was the Baptist minister with whom Sheila and the children stayed in Edinburgh.

Sheila Cloney with Eileen (l) and Mary (r) outside the Longs' house in Edinburgh during the boycott.

The curate, Fr William Stafford (c. 1961), who launched the boycott on 12 May 1957 in Poulfur Church. (Souvenir album: James Staunton, D.D., Bishop of Ferns, 1939–1963)

The Archbishop of Armagh, Cardinal John D'Alton (seated centre left), and the Bishop of Ferns, James Staunton (seated centre right), with members and officials of Wexford Corporation at a ceremony at St Peter's College bestowing the Freedom of Wexford on the cardinal during the Catholic Truth Society congress in June 1957. (Furlong, Nicholas and Hayes, John, County Wexford in the Rare Oul' Times Vol. III, Wexford, 1996)

Seán, Sheila, Eileen and Mary Cloney in the kitchen of Dungulph Castle in January 1958. The newspaper photographer, who took the picture just after the family had returned home on New Year's Eve 1957, manages to capture the sense of anxiety in the Cloney household.

A more relaxed Cloney family standing outside Dungulph Castle almost two years later in September 1959.

Eileen (right) and Mary with baby Hazel in 1962.

Seán Cloney giving a talk at Tintern Abbey in the 1980s.

Seán and Sheila Cloney with three of their grandchildren, (l–r) Brendan, Jeanie and John, in the 1990s.

St Aidan's Church in Poulfur where Fr William Stafford and later Fr Seán Fortune were curates. (Author's photograph)

Main Street, Fethard-on-Sea. (Author's photograph)

greatest encouragement and help.[24] Money also poured in from across Britain – the Orange societies of Scotland were particularly fertile territory – as well as South Africa, Canada, the United States, even Saudi Arabia. It was not just Orangemen who rallied around: members of the Church of Ireland and the other Protestant denominations south of the border also dug into their pockets, as did lay Catholics. Among the latter were those who believed the boycott was an insult to the memory of those who had died fighting for a genuinely pluralist Republic. One donation came from the widow of Terence MacSwiney, Muriel, herself a committed Republican activist, to spend on sweets in the boycotted shops for the local children. Hubert Butler sent the cheque on her behalf, writing that she had 'sympathy for the boycotted as she herself has been badly treated. She left the Catholic Church some years ago and is strongly opposed to the £10,000 memorial fund which is being collected at present to build a memorial chapel to her husband in the Cathedral at Southwark.'[25]

On 13 July, a meeting was held in the tranquil surroundings of Tintern Abbey, a few miles from Fethard, for the purpose of setting up a relief fund to administer the donations. The committee's host and one of the local church elders was the last Colclough to live in Tintern, Lucy Marie Biddulph Colclough. Also present was Lord Templemore, the churchwarden of All Saints Church in Killesk, who had invited Adrian Fisher to become rector of the Fethard Union. Dermot Chichester was the fifth Baron Templemore and was deeply involved in the affairs of the Church of Ireland. He was only forty-one at the time of the boycott, but had already packed a lot into his life. He had attended Harrow and Sandhurst before being commissioned in the 7th Hussars and stationed in Egypt. He was in North Africa when the Second World War broke out and in 1941 was captured fighting in Libya. While being brought to Germany, his train was bombed and he managed to escape before being recaptured. He remained in prison in Italy until 1944 before being released by the camp commandant on the country's surrender, whereupon he went on the run from the Germans until the end of the war. It was 1951 before he returned to settle down in the family home at Dunbrody Park near Arthurstown. Templemore was also the Grand Master of the Freemasons' Grand Lodge of Ireland for ten years after joining the Masonic Lodge in Wexford, as well as being a noted breeder of racehorses. The others in attendance at the meeting were Fisher, the shopkeeper Leslie Gardiner and Shelagh Auld. Fisher was elected treasurer and Auld was elected secretary. The committee first of all tried to estimate the losses of those who were being boycotted. Shelagh Auld's husband, Alex, wrote to Fisher saying he had suffered a loss of £5 a week as the result of Catholics refusing to buy his milk. Another farmer, William Cruise, who had been unable to find labour after falling ill, put his losses over the summer at between £35 and £85. Leslie Gardiner received over £80 from the fund at the beginning of August. By the end of the summer, Fisher was able to report to the committee that the fund had amounted to almost £1,000, out of which £425 had been paid to those affected financially by the boycott.

14

The Secret Deal

At the end of June, the Irish Association of Civil Liberty wrote to Fr Allen, Rev. Adrian Fisher and the five Wexford Dáil deputies asking if they could be of help in ending the boycott. By early July, the association was proposing to send a delegation to Fethard. The association asked Eoin 'the Pope' O'Mahony, who had stood in the general election in Wexford earlier that year, if he would consider being part of the proposed deputation, which would have also included Sean O'Faolain and the senior counsel, Ernest Wood. O'Mahony refused, saying he would rather continue trying to help as a 'freelance'; he had visited Fethard of his own accord and corresponded with Fisher, keeping up to date with much of the gossip about the boycott in Dublin during the summer. In the words of O'Mahony, the association 'cut their own throats' by first visiting Jim Ryan to ask his permission to go to Fethard. Ryan told the delegation, comprising the Earl of Wicklow, T. Desmond Williams

The Fethard-on-Sea Boycott

(Professor of Modern History at University College Dublin), Christopher Gore-Grimes and the honorary secretary, Edgar Deale, that a visit to Fethard 'would not help the situation'. Ryan was himself working behind the scenes to bring the boycott to an end and was of the view that a visit to Fethard from a group of well-intentioned Dublin-based liberals would not help matters. The government was trying to find a way out of the mess without the bishops losing face.

Despite its initially spirited defence of the actions of the boycotters, by the middle of July there was a distinct change in the *Standard*'s editorial stance. It began to urge a resumption of normal relations between the Catholics and Protestants of Fethard. The awful damage being done to the State's reputation for tolerance made continuing support for the boycott unsustainable. The *Standard*, while continuing to argue that the boycott or 'withholding of custom' was a justifiable form of protest, was retreating from its hardline position, while continuing to condemn what it saw as the hypocrisy of Unionist politicians in Northern Ireland.

Meanwhile, Tommy Kelly was also trying to find a way of bringing an end to the boycott. He was shouldering most of the blame from the Catholics for Sheila's disappearance and at that same time was terribly conscious of the suffering of his co-religionists. At the beginning of July, he wrote to the Minister for Justice, Oscar Traynor, requesting that he set up a tribunal to investigate the boycott. Kelly had initially engaged the Taoiseach's son, Terry de Valera, as his solicitor. But de Valera had decided that he could not continue to represent Kelly once his father had intervened in the dispute. Instead, Kelly was represented by David Bell, who drafted the following petition:

The Secret Deal

1. The cause or causes (if ascertainable) which resulted in Sheila Cloney leaving the parish and taking the children.
2. The name of the person or persons (if any) who encouraged her to leave the parish with the children.
3. The name of the person or persons (if any) who subscribed money to her in order that she might maintain herself and her children independently of her husband.
4. The name of the person or persons (if any) who are aware of her present whereabouts or who are in any way assisting her to conceal the children from her husband.
5. And in the event of the Tribunal being satisfied that Sheila Cloney acted not only independently of, but contrary, to the wishes and advice of the members of the Church of Ireland in Fethard-on-Sea, the name of the person or persons who circulated unfounded and reckless rumours.
6. If there is a boycott presently being enforced in Fethard-on-Sea, the extent of same.
7. The name of the person or persons who organised or advocated the boycott.[1]

The petition, which appeared in the newspapers, came with a statement, which called on the Catholics in Fethard to lift the boycott, 'thereby preventing further serious injustices in the parish and the consequent danger to Churches and State'. The statement concluded:

The Fethard-on-Sea Boycott

I feel certain that anyone who thinks, must realise that this boycott can achieve nothing save injustice and it is hardly likely to encourage Sheila Cloney to get in touch with any person in the parish to come back or to send home the children.

In time to come, if not already, this boycott will be regarded as a lamentable chapter in the history of a Christian nation. Let us not only think, but also act like Christians in seeking a solution to this sad and serious problem.

In conclusion, I wish to state that I and all the members of my household are not only available but most anxious to give evidence at such Inquiry.

On 11 July 1957, Peter Berry, the Secretary to the Department of Justice, sent a draft reply to the petition to his counterpart in the Department of the Taoiseach, Maurice Moynihan. In the first paragraph, Berry stated that the Minister had no power to establish such a tribunal. The second paragraph stated that such a tribunal could be set up only by resolution of both Houses of the Oireachtas. However, Berry said he was not sure if this second paragraph should be included in the reply. Moynihan advised Berry to send the reply without the second paragraph.[2]

The secret deal to end the boycott was brokered in Jim Ryan's house in Delgany, County Wicklow. Anthony Hederman, the young barrister engaged by Terry de Valera, who was Tommy Kelly's first solicitor, asked Ryan if he could get members of the vigilance committee in Fethard to a meeting. Hederman had previously tried to engage with Bishop Staunton but without success.

The Secret Deal

Hederman was a staunch Fianna Fáil man. He was a member of the national executive and went on to become Attorney General under Jack Lynch. Ryan invited Jimmy Kennedy and other members of the vigilance committee to Delgany for the meeting. Kennedy and the others were not told about the presence of the barrister when the meeting was arranged. On being told that Hederman was waiting in the study when they arrived, Kennedy was so angry that he came close to leaving. Ryan eased matters by bringing Hederman and Kennedy into his kitchen, whereupon Kennedy recognised Hederman from Fianna Fáil ard fheiseanna. Hederman told Kennedy that the boycott had to be ended. Kennedy agreed but added that the Catholics in Fethard were still convinced there had been a Protestant conspiracy to remove the children from their home. Hederman said he accepted that but warned that he had been given approval from the Archbishop of Dublin to institute civil proceedings against the local church, clergy and members of the vigilance committee. Hederman had asked a clerical friend to see the archbishop to ask for permission to sue the vigilance committee in Fethard. McQuaid had sent the following reply: 'He is a Catholic, and as a Catholic, his primary duty is to ensure that the Catholic Church survives thereby'.[3]

Hederman agreed a deal with Kennedy that in exchange for getting the children home before Christmas, the boycott would end. Kennedy made it clear that there was to be no more talk of the boycott in the press from the Protestants. After the meeting, Hederman contacted the Church of Ireland Archbishop of Dublin, George Otto Simms, who said he would do whatever he could to help find a solution. Hederman told him never to mention Fethard-on-Sea again. Simms agreed. On 7 August, the newspapers reported that an agreement had been reached in the village. Tommy Kelly and Kennedy had met in Dublin the previous day. Kelly and Kennedy, ostensibly representing both sides of the divided community, released the following statement to the press:

> A representative meeting of Catholics and members of the Church of Ireland was held on 6th August, 1957, in Dublin.
>
> On behalf of the Church of Ireland community an undertaking was given by Mr Thomas Kelly to do everything possible to ascertain the whereabouts of the two Cloney children with the averred intention of their restoration to their home.
>
> Mr Kelly deplored the demands of his daughter made on her husband, Mr Seán Cloney.
>
> On behalf of the Catholics Mr James J. Kennedy accepted the undertaking given, and the repudiation.
>
> After a full discussion it was unanimously agreed to publish this statement.[4]

The statement is as interesting for what was left out as for what was included. No mention was made of the boycott, nor was there any admission of culpability on behalf of the local Catholics. It laid the blame firmly with Sheila Cloney and made it clear that it was up to the Church of Ireland community in Fethard to bring her back.

Hederman and Jimmy Kennedy, with the approval of Bishop Staunton, had come up with a formula to extricate the hierarchy from the mess. A draft had been formulated by Hederman and Kennedy and then passed to Staunton for his approval. The bishop made a minor emendation, returned it to Kennedy, who in turn, gave it to Hederman for the approval of his client, Tommy Kelly. All of which had been enabled by Jim Ryan, the Minister for Finance. The Protestants of Fethard were far from pleased. According to Shelagh Auld, the relief fund secretary, the meeting in Dublin had been held without the knowledge of the rector or anybody else in the Church of Ireland in Fethard. 'The general reaction was one of annoyance and disapproval as none of us was guilty of giving Mrs Cloney financial support to go away and we as a Community were ignorant of her pending departure, and as we still know nothing of her whereabouts, we consider it is a family affair,' she wrote in a letter to the barrister Alexander M. Sullivan on 13 August. She continued:

> We feel we are entitled to a public apology from the instigators of the boycott, rather than trying to come to terms with them. However, in the interest of those of us who are most affected by the boycott, personal feelings have been suppressed for the time being until we see if there is any appreciable change in the situation.[5]

The Protestants of Fethard had every reason to be aggrieved. As Shelagh Auld pointed out, none of them knew of Sheila Cloney's whereabouts or had offered her any financial assistance, but they were being persecuted for allegedly conniving to have her spirited away from her husband.

The Fethard-on-Sea Boycott

Sullivan was the younger son of the more eminent A. M. Sullivan, a lawyer from Bantry in County Cork who had been editor of *The Nation*, a Westminster MP and a leading light in the temperance movement (his wife was a co-founder of the Total Abstinence Association of the Sacred Heart, founded in Gardiner Street in Dublin in 1898). The younger Sullivan, who was eighty-six at the time of the boycott, had also had an interesting career. He was the last Irish serjeant-at-law – the highest rank of barrister at the English and Irish bar until its dissolution – and was the leading counsel for the defence at the trial for treason of Roger Casement in 1916. Shelagh Auld duly acknowledged Sullivan's offer of assistance to the relief fund.

The press described 'a new air of hope' in the village following the publication of the statement. The *Standard* welcomed the statement, which it said was 'in harmony with what we have already written', and trusted the undertaking would 'bear fruit'. Adrian Fisher, who was shown a copy by a reporter, gave the statement a cautious welcome but remarked that it would a take a few days for things to settle down.[6] He said that it would be 'a great day for Ireland' when the boycott was over. Fr Allen was less positive. He said that 'we understood that there was to be no more publicity or letters about it following the statement, and it would be better if no more were written. It is better to give it a little time. The publicity this has got has given people outside the wrong impression. It was grossly exaggerated. The less said about it now, the better it will be.'[7]

On 10 August, *The Irish Times* reported that the Protestant traders had regained none of their lost customers and that it was felt that only 'a direct statement by the local Catholic clergy will bring about an improvement in the situation'. Betty Cooper told the paper that before the boycott 'she had a very good trade in novels and magazines, but it has practically disappeared. It will probably take years to build it up again.'[8] There was no reference to the boycott or the statement the next day at Sunday Mass. As far as the boycott was concerned, it was business – or no business – as usual.

The deal was a bitter pill for the Fethard Protestants to swallow. They were still suffering the consequences of the boycott. They were being linked to efforts to find Sheila Cloney, despite consistently stating that they had no part in her disappearance and regarded it as solely the affair of the family. Some members of the vigilance committee also had trouble accepting the statement, believing that the fight should be continued until the Cloney children were returned. But faced with the threat of legal action, pressure from the higher powers in Fianna Fáil and a disapproving de Valera, Kennedy was shrewd enough to realise that the jig was up. It was now a question of letting the Catholics in Fethard get used to the fact.

The local newspapers had carried little news about the boycott during the summer. In its edition of 10 August, the *People* reported that a school of thirty-six killer whales (or orcas) had swum into the harbour at Fethard that week. The whales had come in on a full tide in about ten feet of water 'like a mighty fleet becalmed' before 'spouting mighty gusts of brine and churning the water in a frenzied cauldron'. The next day they were motionless. The whales had missed the tide and were dying. Fishermen cut up the dead whales to sell as meal for animals. Hundreds of onlookers stood watching at the dock. It was a bizarre if perhaps welcome respite from the tensions of the summer.

As had been promised, the Protestant hierarchy ceased to mention the boycott and it gradually disappeared from the newspapers. But while it was no longer front-page news, the boycott did not really come to an end. By 12 September, the *Belfast Telegraph*, which continued to investigate the tribulations of the Fethard Protestants when other papers had stopped doing so, reported that a few Catholics had returned to Leslie Gardiner's shop but that 'otherwise the situation was just as before'. Two weeks later, the same newspaper reported that Fr Allen had gone in to Gardiner's to settle his outstanding account and buy a packet of cigarettes. This symbolic act was a signal that there would no longer be a sanction on those who chose to return to the Protestant shops. But many never did.

Eric Waugh, who had reported from Fethard for the *Belfast Telegraph* throughout the summer, wrote that the parish priest's gesture was being 'interpreted as the proferring of an olive branch' and that 'there is no doubt that the atmosphere in the village is easier now than at any time since the flight of Mrs Sheila Cloney with her two children'. Visiting Fr Allen for the same article, Waugh reported that the priest stood at the window of the parochial house looking across the fields in the direction of Fethard a few miles away, saying: 'I thought that trouble was all over down there – I can't understand what all the publicity is about.'

By the end of September, a few Catholics were returning to the Protestant shops – those no doubt who were ashamed at the hurt, both financial and emotional, they had caused their neighbours but who had been cowed by the clergy and their lay lieutenants into upholding the boycott. According to Waugh, 'the self-appointed vigilance committee which administered the boycott in Fethard on military lines had ceased to meet'.[9] But progress was slow. Some Catholics never returned to the two Protestant shops. The relief fund, under the chairmanship of Rev. Fisher, was still in operation and receiving letters requesting assistance. Some £1,300 had been subscribed and several hundred pounds paid out. At the end of October, the *Church of Ireland Gazette* returned to events in Fethard, having made no comment since the turbulent days of July. It reported that the boycott was 'still on' and that the 'much-publicised' statement of Tommy Kelly and Jimmy Kennedy had 'not, so far as can be ascertained, done more than deceive the public outside the area into thinking that all is now well'. The *Gazette* revealed the indignation of local Protestants, who considered the statement signed by Tommy Kelly and Jimmy Kennedy 'constituted a complete betrayal of their position':

> We refrained at the time from comment on what appeared to us to be a very one-sided and, so far as the Church of Ireland position was concerned, apologetic document. We did so in the hope that, faces thus being saved, the spirit of Christian charity might be allowed to do its work. Things have not happed this way, and we would be doing less than our duty to our own people were we to allow them to remain in ignorance of the true position.[10]

The Fethard-on-Sea Boycott

On New Year's Eve 1957, more than eight months after leaving Dungulph Castle, Sheila Cloney returned home with her two children. She told reporters it was 'good to be back home'. By an odd series of events she had first learned of the boycott from some evangelical literature that had arrived on the Orkney Islands from Peru. The family with whom she was staying on the Orkneys – to where she had moved with the children from Edinburgh – were associated with a global network of missionaries. One of their missions was in Peru. The mission there had highlighted the intolerance of the Catholic Church, using the story about the boycott in *Time* magazine and included the article in a letter which ended up in the house where she was staying. Sheila then wrote to her husband who wrote back saying he would come to the Orkneys as soon as he could. On 1 November, the couple were reunited. Seán met Sheila in Kirkwall, the main island, before they travelled the last leg of the journey together to Westray, the northernmost island, to be reunited with the children. Seán stayed there for three weeks. From the Orkneys they went to Somerset where Seán worked on a farm. At the end of 1957 they returned to Wexford.

Returning home was difficult for the Cloneys. The couple were still newsworthy and the newspapers swarmed to Fethard soon after Sheila's return. Unable to cope with the pressure, Sheila and the children crossed to Fishguard in Wales just over two weeks after returning. They rented a mobile home which Seán visited at the weekends. The family did not return again until Easter 1958. Meanwhile, the matter of the school was left unresolved. Sending the children to either the Catholic or the Protestant school would have caused too much resentment either way. So Eileen and Mary were educated at home.

For the Protestants in the village, things were never the same again. At the beginning of 1958, one of the shopkeepers told a local newspaper, 'Only a few of my old customers have come back. It is terrible. I had hoped everything would be forgotten when Mrs Cloney came back.'[11] Another newspaper reported that 'some of the Fethard Catholics still persist in their unkind attitude towards their Protestant neighbours'.[12] It was to take the efforts of a later generation to start the painful process of reconciliation.

15

The Aftermath

The boycott had a lasting impact on both the
Catholic Church and the Church of Ireland, the
reputation of the Irish State and, of course, on the
relationship between the Catholics and Protestants of
Fethard. For the Catholic Church, the boycott had been an
unequivocal disaster. It had been forced to withdraw its
support for the boycott before the Cloney children had
returned to Fethard. The hierarchy quickly began to mull
over its mistakes.

Bishop Staunton, who had the greatest stake in a
successful outcome to the boycott, believed the main
problem was that the Church had lost the propaganda
battle. On 21 January 1958, in a letter to Archbishop
McQuaid, he wrote that the Church had failed to argue its
case successfully. This attitude was shared by others within
the hierarchy who believed that Protestants had become
adept at managing public opinion, while the Catholic laity

The Aftermath

sat on its hands. Staunton wrote to McQuaid that 'Protestant propaganda, in my opinion successful, was in fact an attack on the Catholic Church, under the guise of an attack on the people of Fethard-on-Sea, and I felt strongly the want of an organisation, not to defend the people of Fethard-on-Sea, but to put the facts, which I could supply, before the public'. The Mother-and-Child controversy and the widespread criticism of the bishops' support for the boycott led Staunton to believe that the direction of public opinion and the defence of Catholic interests through the press was a priority for the Church. 'The lay public, in *general*, accept without criticism, or even any thought, what they read, including, in too many cases, attacks on the Catholic Church, its teaching and leaders,'[1] he wrote.

One of the problems facing the hierarchy was that Catholic laymen were afraid to pick up a pen in defence of the Church in case they were out of kilter with the bishops. But the public relations failures of the 1950s found the hierarchy keen to instigate greater lay action in defence of Catholic morals from the perceived threat of modernism and secularism. The boycott accelerated the debate about the establishment of a public relations bureau (see Appendix).

Bishops Staunton and Browne failed to achieve their objectives during the boycott. Staunton failed to extend the boycott beyond the Hook peninsula. De Valera's rejection of the boycott was fundamental to this failure, but it was Archbishop McQuaid's tacit acknowledgement that de Valera could not let the boycott go unchecked that undermined the boycotters. McQuaid recognised that de Valera saw the boycott as fundamentally unjust and hugely harmful to the national reputation. After McQuaid had signed off on de Valera's statement in the Dáil, it was a question of finding a way to end the boycott while letting the Catholic Church save face.

The boycott may be seen as a divergence between Church and State, of which there were very few in the first four decades of independent Ireland. On the other hand, de Valera had always compartmentalised his own religious faith and loyalty to the Church from his political beliefs and from what he perceived as the best interests of the State. He believed that the State should interfere as little as possible within what he recognised as the church's moral and social sphere of influence. But he believed the reverse also held true when it came to what he saw as the State's sphere of influence, as evidenced by his rejection of the Church and the opposition's frenzied calls for Ireland to throw its weight behind Franco's forces against the democratically elected Republican government during the Spanish Civil War.

De Valera's immediate inclination, once the boycott had become national news, was to write to Bishop Staunton in the strongest possible terms. He was understandably upset that the country's reputation for religious tolerance – which had been bolstered by the hugely successful tour of the United States by the Jewish Lord Mayor of Dublin, Bob Briscoe – had been fundamentally undermined by the actions of a solitary priest. This reputation for tolerance was built on very shaky foundations. Nevertheless, de Valera's government was able to argue that Protestants had nothing to fear from a united Ireland, whereas Catholics suffered terrible discrimination from the Unionist government of Northern Ireland. His own attitudes and his somewhat misguided belief that the Republic was not a cold place for

The Aftermath

Protestants convinced de Valera of the futility and injustice of the boycott. But it was the fact that one of the strongest anti-partition arguments – that the Republic was a haven for religious tolerance compared to the nakedly sectarian North – had been undermined that was the greatest determining factor in his decision to speak out.

To northern Protestants, the boycott was proof, if any were needed, of what they could expect in a United Ireland: persecution at the hands of Roman Catholic priests. The Fethard boycott was used by scaremongering anti-Catholic propagandists such as Ian Paisley, who built his career on bashing 'Romanists', and Norman Porter, who was instrumental in raising large sums of money for the relief of the Fethard Protestants. They railed against the tyranny of the Republic. But, while the shouts of defiance from Protestant leaders were deafening in the North, in the South the Church of Ireland chose to say nothing.

The writer Hubert Butler, one of the great scourges of hypocrisy in 1950s' Ireland, believed that Fethard was a turning point in the history of the Church of Ireland. In his view, the failure of southern Protestants to stand up to the bullying of the Catholic Church was a tragic missed opportunity, the last chance of 'a direct confrontation with *Ne Temere*'. In 1973, he wrote:

> All we had to do to bring the boycott to an immediate close was to give vigorous support to the victims of a manifest injustice, as would have been our duty, whether the boycotted were Catholic or Protestant.
>
> There were thousands of Protestants in Waterford, Wexford and Kilkenny, and in two days there could

have been such an avalanche of assistance as would have landed the boycotted in security for the rest of their days.[2]

Butler believed that 'a great common gesture' at the time of the boycott would have 'given us courage and confidence and arrested the sad slow Protestant decline'. It was a view shared by many of his co-religionists. There was a sense that the Church of Ireland in the Republic had shown great weakness by refusing to stand up to the Catholic Church. Instead of defending the Protestants of Fethard, the elderly Bishop Phair advised them to turn the other cheek. He blamed the boycott on Sheila Cloney, mixed marriages and coverage in the press. His criticism of the Catholic clergy and hierarchy was muted. He declined to request meetings with Bishop Staunton. Noisy northern Unionists with their own political agendas had filled the vacuum, much to the disgust of southern Protestants, who felt that their own leaders had deserted them. Butler wrote that it seemed to him that 'Protestant leaders were trying to buy us off our duty with cheques and as though the welfare of some shopkeepers and dairy farmers was at stake and not our children's freedom and the Protestant right of private judgment'.[3]

The damage caused by the *Ne Temere* decree to the Church of Ireland was immense. It resulted in fewer and fewer children in Church of Ireland pews on Sundays, a reduced income for the parish, and the closure of Protestant-run schools. In the mid-1990s, one senior Protestant churchman compared the *Ne Temere* decree to 'social genocide'.[4]

The Aftermath

The former Protestant national school on Fethard's main street is now derelict, though an engraved sign is still visible on the outside wall. It went the way of the two small Catholic national schools at Loftus Hall and Templetown, which were amalgamated with the national school at Poulfur in the 1960s. The Garda barracks in Fethard also closed, as did most of the shops and pubs in the village that had existed at the time of the boycott. But memories of the boycott remain strong in Fethard.

Eileen Cloney was six when her mother took her and her sister away to Belfast. She does not remember much about the city. One vivid memory is that of playing with her sister Mary in the garden outside a house. Her mother was talking to people inside and she remembers throwing stones at the window. Her next memory is running up the gangway onto a boat. The gangway was at the docks in Dublin. The boat was going to Liverpool. From Liverpool, they travelled to Edinburgh, then to Westray. She remembers her father coming to visit them on the island in November 1957.

The boycott was supposed to have fizzled out by the time Sheila Cloney returned home. But Fr Stafford, who remained as curate in Poulfur until 1962, evidently did not feel the debate about Eileen's schooling was over. Once the Cloneys had returned home, he came again to Dungulph Castle and behaved as if nothing had happened. He entered the kitchen, asked about Seán, who was ill upstairs in bed, went up to see him and then left. Stafford was still putting pressure on Seán to send Eileen to the Catholic school at Poulfur. Instead, Eileen was educated at home. 'We kept to ourselves, didn't play with the local children, we'd have to stay sitting in the car when we went to the village,' she recalled in 1999. 'I was seventeen before I got out at all. I never went to school . . . No Inter Cert, no Leaving Cert, nothing. It was harder on Mary; she never went at all. I think everybody was quite willing to forget about us after all that happened, but we lost out badly. We never felt that we were on equal standing with other people, because we had no education.'[5]

On another occasion, after a tongue-lashing from the clergy, Seán told Sheila that the children had to go to Mass. But Sheila stood firm and the following Sunday drove Eileen and Mary a few miles from home to a gateway. There the three of them waited until Mass was over. When it was time to go, she discovered she had a puncture, so she had to drive home with the tyre flat on the rim. Curiously enough, Seán and Sheila's youngest daughter, Hazel, who was born in 1961 and baptised in the Church of Ireland, was sent to the Catholic school in Poulfur, much to her sisters' surprise. But Hazel also had to learn to deal with local people's memories of the boycott.

Reconciliation came slowly to Fethard. But a poignant occasion six years after the boycott showed there was cause for hope. Seán recalled it forty years later:

> Sheila's brother had two children with holes in their hearts. They went to Guy's Hospital in London and one of them, a little girl of three, died. Sheila had two sisters married to Catholics and when the child came home three Catholics carried the little coffin up the avenue to the Protestant church. At the time, Catholics were forbidden to enter a Protestant church and there were men at the door to take the coffin.

The Aftermath

The little coffin had a three-year-old child in it, our niece. I went into the church and the other two men followed suit. When they saw that, other Catholics came in. It was a milestone.[6]

Two men – Fr Richard Hayes, the curate at Poulfur, and Rev. Jimmy Grant – did much to heal the wounds in the village. The solution of the two clerics to the bad feeling that still existed between the two sides was eminently sensible. They used to go to a local pub and have a drink together. Hayes was appointed curate in 1964 following the departure of his predecessor, James Byrne. Stafford had been transferred to Duncannon on the west side of the Hook where he served as curate for a number of years. In 1970, he became parish priest at Kilaveney in County Wicklow. He died in 1980.

Over the years, small symbols of unity helped to heal the village, such as when the GAA needed to clear a debt on its local ground and the Church of Ireland was looking to raise funds for a new roof for the local church. So they came together to raise the funds. But progress was slow and it took about twenty years in Seán Cloney's estimation before he was rehabilitated in the eyes of many of his Catholic neighbours. Then, in 1981, the arrival of another Catholic priest in Poulfur brought yet more division. The new priest was a native of Gorey in the north of the county who had initially been posted to Belfast. But problems with his fellow clergy led to the local bishop transferring him out of his diocese. On 31 August 1981, he was appointed curate in Poulfur. His name was Seán Fortune. When he first arrived, Fortune sought to take control of the parish hall.

The Fethard-on-Sea Boycott

This was the same parish hall that had caused the trouble in the 1940s between Fr Stafford and his parish priest, Canon Thomas Cloney, Seán Cloney's uncle – and the same hall from which Fr Stafford banished Seán Cloney because he was going out with a Protestant woman. By the 1970s the hall was in debt and Fr Hayes, who had done so much to promote good ecumenical relations in the parish, asked Seán Cloney to become the chairman of the parish hall committee. When Fr Fortune tried to take control of the hall, he found Seán Cloney in his way. Fortune did not manage to get his grip on the hall but he did manage to split the village.

Fortune was also a paedophile. Thanks to some first-rate investigative journalism, his suicide and the damning indictment of the 2005 report of the government inquiry into child sex abuse in the diocese of Ferns, the truth is now out. But in the 1980s, the children he was abusing were not being heard. Many in positions of authority abdicated their responsibilities at a time when clerical child abuse did not officially exist in Ireland. Those who knew what was happening and attempted to bring it to the attention of the authorities were too often ignored.

It was in 1984, at the height of Fortune's tyranny, that I first visited Fethard on my summer holidays with my uncle, aunt and cousins who were over from England. Shortly after we arrived at Dungulph Castle, which the Cloneys rented out during the summer months, Seán Cloney advised my father and my uncle that under no circumstances should any of the children be brought anywhere near Poulfur. He told them that if they wanted to go to Mass, they should go instead to Templetown. Cloney compiled a large file of evidence relating to Fortune's abuse of children and alerted the Bishop of Ferns, Brendan Comiskey, to the priest's crimes throughout the 1980s.

Despite his battles with Fortune and the damage it did to his relations with some of his Catholic neighbours, Seán Cloney did not lose his sense of humour. The summer of 1985 was the time of the moving statues. The country was in a religious fervour. In July, two teenage girls in the west Cork village of Ballinspittle reported seeing a statue of the Virgin Mary move. The grotto, like thousands of others in housing estates, villages and towns across Ireland, had been built to celebrate the Marian Year in 1954. Within days, thousands of pilgrims had travelled to Ballinspittle in the hope of seeing the statue move. Each night, the faithful would come to pray and many claimed they had seen the expression on the Virgin's face change or the statue rock. Camera crews and journalists descended on the village. Soon people were reportedly seeing statues of the Virgin move in shrines across the country. The airwaves were flooded with witnesses who had seen moving statues. One 37-year-old woman who had been deaf since the age of twenty claimed her hearing had been restored after a visit to the Ballinspittle grotto. The sceptics and believers joined debate as to whether this was mass hysteria or a miraculous phenomenon. Back in Fethard, Fr Fortune decided that a moving statue would be good for business and tried to encourage a miracle in Poulfur. 'In spite of a considerable degree of pressure by the local curate on some children to bear witness that they had seen a Poulfur statue "move" or whatever,' Seán Cloney mused at the time, 'the enterprise proved unsuccessful and it was decided that the statue must be considered "Out of Order" or at any rate, most uncooperative!'

In 1987, Seán Cloney gave an interview to the *Sunday Press* on the thirtieth anniversary of the boycott. He had remained a regular Mass-goer. During the course of the article, the reporter mentioned that Sheila would go to St Mogue's every Sunday morning, while her husband would bypass Poulfur Church, close to his home, in favour of Templetown, a good few miles the other side of Fethard. Seán tended to be diplomatic in interviews. But during the course of his chat with the reporter Michael Bance, he struck a note of rare anger: 'The best advice I ever got was from a priest in a religious order who told me to shut the gate when my wife and children were home and never let a priest, minister or bishop of any denomination past it.'[7] By the end of 1987, Fortune was gone. He was officially embarking on a media studies course in London. The people of Fethard picked themselves up once more, and learned to live with Fortune's cruel legacy.

In 1995, misfortune struck the Cloney family again when Seán was involved in a traffic accident near Ferrycarrig, outside Wexford town. When an ambulance arrived, he walked to it and was taken to Wexford General Hospital. He was not suffering any significant pain. An X-ray showed that he had a hairline fracture in the bone of his neck.

The following morning he was transferred to hospital in Dublin, to be fitted with a halo brace. This involved affixing a metal ring to the skull by means of four screws and fitting a metal section to the neck and shoulders to hold the head in a fixed position. But something went badly wrong and he suffered damage to his spinal cord. He underwent major surgery, but it was unsuccessful and he was left paralysed from the neck down. Seán Cloney spent three years in the National Rehabilitation Hospital in Dún Laoghaire. Some people whispered that this was the kind of thing that happened when you 'went agin the priest'.

In a strange twist of fate, Seán Cloney was to cross paths with Fortune once more. In March 1999, the 45-year-old priest was found dead by his housekeeper at his home in New Ross. He was lying on his back on his bed, his hands joined and holding a set of rosary beads. Beside his bed was a poem entitled 'A message from heaven to my family', and an empty bottle of whiskey in a wastepaper basket. The net had been closing in on Fortune. The previous week he had faced twenty-nine charges of sexual abuse against eight young boys in Wexford Circuit Court during the years he had been curate at Poulfur. During the case, the judge said it had become apparent that there was a question concerning the priest's competence. The judge had remanded him to the Central Mental Hospital for treatment but there was a strike on there and so he was sent to Mountjoy Prison instead. He was granted bail in the High Court the following Monday. Five days later he killed himself. The inquest found that Fortune had died from cardio-respiratory failure owing to an overdose of drugs washed down with whiskey. His house, replete with altar, lectern, chalice and candles, had been barricaded with steel shutters and security cameras monitored for signs of intruders. The newspapers filled pages with the fantastical nature of his death. Reporters travelled to Fethard looking for more sensational copy. One old adversary must have spent those frenetic few days in the aftermath of the priest's death reflecting on the strange hand life had dealt him. Seán Cloney was in Wexford Regional Hospital receiving treatment when he was brought the news: Seán Fortune was dead. His corpse was lying downstairs in the mortuary.

Seán Cloney continued to devote his time to the study of local history. The 1798 Rebellion was one of his main interests. He was involved in the bicentennial commemorations in 1998, acting as the historical adviser to Comóradh, the Wexford commemorative committee, which, among other activities, was responsible for the Scullabogue memorial unveiled that year in the Church of Ireland graveyard in Old Ross. He was also a regular contributor to the journals of the Wexford Historical Society. In 1998, during an ecumenical service in Wexford as part of the 1798 Rebellion bicentennial commemorations, the Bishop of Ferns, Brendan Comiskey, expressed 'deep sorrow' for the part the Catholic Church had played in the affair. In the presence of his Church of Ireland counterpart, the Bishop of Cashel and Ossory, John Neill, he noted that it was 'a very public and historic occasion' and said:

> I am acutely conscious of one very painful episode in our history, an incident which occurred 41 years ago this very month and which is referred to in our history books as 'the Fethard-on-Sea Boycott'.
>
> Today, if at all possible. I wish to bring healing and closure to this sad period in our history by expressing my deep sorrow and my promise to do whatever I can to make amends. In the presence of Bishop John Neill and his predecessor, Bishop Noel Willoughby, I ask

forgiveness and healing from God, from all within the Church of Ireland community, and from all who have suffered in any way then or since.[8]

Seán Cloney welcomed the apology on RTÉ news later that night but said it was 'a source of regret that it has taken forty-one years'. He added: 'I would like to publicly thank Bishop Comiskey for undoing what other members of the Hierarchy did in 1957.' Five days later Bishop Comiskey, in an article published in *The Irish Times*, wrote that his reasons for making the Pentecost Sunday apology were in great part personal: 'When I most needed support, no one of any religious persuasion was more generous and forthcoming than members of the Church of Ireland in this diocese, people like Ivan Yates TD, Bishops Noel Willoughby and John Neill, the Rev. Nigel Waugh and so many others, clergy and laity.'[9]

On 18 October 1999, Seán Cloney died in Wexford Regional Hospital at the age of seventy-three. Five months before his death, he attended the premiere of *A Love Divided*, the cinematic adaptation of the boycott story. Producer Gerry Gregg had conceived of the project after interviewing Hubert Butler in 1990 for *Sheep May Safely Graze*, an RTÉ documentary about the Protestant experience in independent Ireland. Butler had convinced Gregg that the Fethard-on-Sea Boycott was a seminal moment in the emergence of modern Ireland. Actors Liam Cunningham and Orla Brady played Seán and Sheila Cloney in the film. Cunningham's Seán is a rough-hewn sort of fellow – far removed from the warm, witty man brimming with intellectual curiosity that friends and family remember. Gregg acknowledged that he had taken dramatic licence with Seán's character in order to simplify the story for the big screen and portray Orla Brady's Sheila as the hero of the piece. Gregg explained this to Seán, who, typically, was understanding.

Seán Cloney was not a man to be bitter. He retained his dry sense of humour throughout his travails and, in retrospect, rather enjoyed the fact that he had been at the centre of this infamous episode in Irish history. He had lived to hear the Catholic Church apologise for its actions during the boycott. He remained a practising Catholic, despite the great difficulties his opposition to the boycott – and later to Fr Fortune – were to cause him. He is buried in the same grave as his father and mother beside Templetown Church. The inscription upon his gravestone reads: 'Misfortunes will happen to the wisest and best of men.' Immediately opposite is the grave of Fr Allen.

Eileen Cloney still lives close to Fethard. She shares her father's sense of humour and is not bitter about what befell her. She has a love of painting and is working on restoring the watermill at Dungulph, another passion of her father's. In 1999, she was deputed as family spokesman during the publicity that surrounded the release of A Love Divided. It was a particularly difficult year for the family. Mary had died the year before from a rare liver disease, leaving behind a husband and two children. She had specified her own funeral arrangements, which involved the two religious traditions in which she had been brought up. The Church of Ireland rector of the New Ross union of parishes, into which Fethard had been amalgamated, said prayers before Mary's remains were removed from the funeral home in

The Aftermath

Wellingtonbridge to the Catholic church at Poulfur before her burial in the little Church of Ireland graveyard beside St Mogue's. The rector, Paul Mooney, was a former Catholic priest who had left the Church to get married and was then ordained in the Church of Ireland.

Hazel Cloney also still lives close to Fethard. Born in 1961, four years after the boycott, she was the only one of the three Cloney girls to attend school – and a Catholic school at that, despite being baptised in the Church of Ireland – but was conscious of being somewhat different from her peers because of the strange events that had occurred before she was born. Despite not being alive at the time of the boycott, the course of her life was profoundly altered by the events of 1957.

Sheila wished to draw a veil over the boycott all her life and could never see the sense of talking about the past, despite the fact that many of her neighbours still viewed her in the light of her actions on that April day in 1957. She continued to live in a bungalow beside Dungulph Castle until her death on 28 June 2009. Her funeral service was held in the tiny St Mogue's Church. It was a low-key affair: there was no eulogy, no death notices in the newspapers. Sheila had given careful instructions; she did not want any fuss. It was typical of the woman. She had striven for an ordinary life. Her parents had raised her to value family, hard work and being a good neighbour. She gave freely of her spare time to the Church of Ireland. The immaculately kept graveyard which frames St Mogue's is a tribute to her work. She is now buried there with Mary.

Sheila is the heroine of the story. She was stubborn and headstrong. Many strong women would have given way in the face of the clergy's incessant bullying, but Sheila did not accept that Catholic priests had the right to interfere in her family's lives. And by doing so, she struck a small blow against the moral tyranny of the Catholic Church in 1950s' Ireland. For that she should be remembered.

Appendix: The Catholic Public Relations Bureau

I n June, at the height of the boycott, an advisory committee, which had been established to study ways in which lay Catholics could be encouraged to defend the Church's position in the newspapers, issued its report to the bishops. It recommended setting up a documentation centre containing, among other reference sources, newspaper cuttings, periodicals and directories to enable members of the laity and clergy to arm themselves before joining battle with the Church's enemies in the columns of the press. The committee also felt that the hierarchy should issue a statement on the duties of Catholics in 'the formation of a healthy public opinion' and more positively encourage 'the efforts of priests and laymen of ability' in expressing their Catholic viewpoints since there was 'a widespread belief that any activity not specifically authorised would be either unwarranted or unwelcome'.[1] It was believed that while Protestants were criticising the

Church through such organs as *The Irish Times*, good
Catholics were refraining from defending her for fear of
being out of kilter with the official line.

The committee was unanimous in its belief that greater
effort was required from the laity in defending the Church.
But when it came to a proposed public relations bureau,
there was disagreement. The majority report concluded: 'As
regards the question of a Public Relations Bureau, we feel
that the expression of opinion is more effective if it is
spontaneous and not officially inspired, and that a Public
Relations Bureau would be likely to acquire in the mind of
the public a quasi-official character and thereby create new
problems.' Any further steps in this regard, the report
added, should be taken only in the light of the experience
gained as a result of implementing the other recommendations. The bishops had also asked the committee to come
up with a list of names suitable for a panel that would be on
call to counteract negative criticism of the church. The
majority of the committee were equally uneasy about such
a panel. They wrote that 'those whose names were not
included in this panel might be discouraged from playing
their part in the formation of public opinion'.[2] In
submitting a list, they confined themselves 'to indicating
the type of person whose services might be availed of'.
Among the names appended to the majority report were the
Queens' University academic Monsignor Arthur Ryan; the
Irish Independent columnist John D. Sheridan; the long-
serving UCC Professor of History James Hogan; the
historian Denis Gwynn; and the former President of UCC,
Alfred O'Rahilly, who had taken holy orders two years
previously.

Appendix: The Catholic Public Relations Bureau

Two members of the committee, Fr Peter Birch and Fr Jeremiah Newman, both of whom were later ordained bishops, dissented from the majority opinion. They argued that a centrally directed public relations group 'may be necessary in present circumstances to counter the effects produced by anti-Catholic propaganda and by inadequate presentation of Catholic interests'. They continued: 'We submit respectfully, therefore, as our opinion that an informal group of competent young men, centrally situated and preferably lay, would be of benefit for this purpose. We think that those chosen should already have given indications of ability and willingness to act in this capacity, and that they should be known besides for independence and integrity.'[3] Birch and Newman submitted their own list of names. These were Fr James Kavanagh of UCD, subsequently an auxiliary Bishop of Dublin; Fr Michael O'Neill, a Columban priest; Patrick Kilroy, a solicitor and member of the Catholic Truth Society; Seamus Grace of the Legion of Mary; and another *Irish Independent* journalist, Francis D'Arcy.

It seems the hierarchy was more impressed by the views of Birch and Newman than by their colleagues with regard to the proposed bureau and the best means of encouraging the laity to argue the Catholic viewpoints, perhaps regarding them as more appropriate to the establishment of a modern public relations machinery. During their general meeting of 25 June, the bishops decided to accept Birch and Newman's minority report. Bishop Staunton and the Bishop of Raphoe, William McNeely, were chosen to act as a liaison between the hierarchy and the new group. In September 1957, the Committee on Documentation and

Public Opinion was established. As recommended in the minority report, the membership included Fr Kavanagh, who served as chairman, Fr O'Neill, Kilroy and Grace. Birch, Edward Power and Leon Ó Bróin (then Secretary of the Department of Posts and Telegraphs and, later, author of many books on Irish history) were also co-opted. The new committee had two stated terms of reference. The first was the establishment of a Catholic documentation centre. The second was to encourage 'intelligent lay Catholics to write on matters of interest to the Church and thereby help to develop an enlightened public opinion'. In its preliminary report, issued on 8 January 1958, the committee advised the hierarchy that it had established an 'informal group of laymen who will actively participate in public controversy and meet regularly to discuss problems of Catholic interest'. The committee proposed:

(1) That only persons of the highest integrity and independent mind should be invited to join the group.

(2) That the group must be completely independent of the Committee and preferably not aware of its existence.

(3) That the Committee cannot be responsible for the views expressed by any member of the group, the independence of which is considered essential.[4]

The committee believed that 'fear of ecclesiastical censure' prevented laymen from writing in defence of Catholic principles and 'hoped that the laymen selected will overcome this fear through the encouragement of their fellow members in the group'.[5]

The committee's recommendations to the hierarchy signalled a recognition that the mood in the country was slowly changing. No longer was it good enough to give dissidents a swift belt of the crozier. In order to promote the Catholic viewpoint, it was necessary to give the laity some leeway to express themselves. Events over the last decade, beginning with the Mother-and-Child controversy, had shown that the Catholic Church was no longer unassailable. The bishops could not count on the unquestioning obeisance of the Catholic population. The shrewder among them recognised that to alienate committed Catholics was unhelpful. Others, however, were more interested in fighting a rearguard action against the diminution of their own power.

The hierarchy discussed the report at what was described by Bishop Staunton as 'a very pregnant' meeting of their standing committee on 14 January 1958.[6] The bishops were not pleased. Bishop Fergus of Achonry wrote to the secretary of the public relations committee, Patrick Kilroy, that the hierarchy was at a loss to explain why the report had pointed out repeatedly the need for independent thinkers in the group. 'While it goes without saying that such a group should consist of persons of the highest integrity, it was not clear to Their Lordships what was involved in the suggestion that this is a point which required to be further considered and clarified.'[7] Ironically, given the report's emphasis on easing the climate of fear that existed among the Catholic laity, the bishops' reply frightened the members of the public relations' committee.

Bishops Staunton and McNeely had already met the committee members on 14 January to try to close the gap between the attitudes of the committee and the bishops. Staunton reported on the meeting in a letter to Archbishop McQuaid the next day. His words are revealing of McQuaid's power within the hierarchy. 'I recommended that Father Kavanagh should call upon your Grace, that you were the only one who could settle this problem, that you were accustomed to settling problems, and that you would settle this problem for them if it were possible.'

On 7 February, McQuaid met the committee members to soothe their frazzled nerves. In a note to McQuaid after the meeting, Fr Kavanagh wrote of how much of a relief it was to have his direction. Speaking of his committee colleagues, Kavanagh wrote: 'They were all immensely pleased and encouraged. They went home as happy as schoolchildren. They are, I believe, a very capable group, but they needed a little pat on the back. Your Grace's very cordial and sympathetic treatment of them has been a wonderful tonic (not least for the poor chairman [Kavanagh himself]).'[8]

McQuaid's thoughts on the meeting, as expressed in a memorandum on the meeting, are equally revealing. He wrote of the committee's 'worries and fears of being brought to book by Bishops for mistakes in their apostolate'. As regards the letter from the Bishop of Achonry, McQuaid told the committee that it only revealed 'a puzzled group of Bishops' and was not meant as a criticism. Somewhat bizarrely, McQuaid advised the committee to reply to the concerns of his fellow bishops by indicating 'that "Independent" in their view meant just "responsible".' He

Appendix: The Catholic Public Relations Bureau

added that he had 'urged that they go ahead as my own diocesans . . . whose mistakes I will certainly overlook, for no mistakes will be of malice'. McQuaid also rowed in behind the committee's belief that a modern documentation centre was needed, contrary to the views of his fellow bishops on the standing committee. 'One is pushing an open door, in urging these and like men to work for the church. But there is a palsy of fear on laymen who wish to be apostolic,' he concluded.[9]

Acknowledgements

I wish first and foremost to thank the Cloney family for their unceasing generosity. Ever since I embarked on this project, they have gone out of their way to provide whatever assistance they could. This book could not have been written without their help. My thanks are also due to Adrian and Liz Fanning who invited my parents and myself to join them on holiday in Dungulph Castle in the early 1980s where I first heard about the boycott. I am grateful to Adrian and Pan Fisher for sharing their memories of the boycott and showing me great hospitality in their house in Henley-on-Thames. David Gardiner's depiction of his father, Leslie, and his teenage memories of Fethard in 1957 were most illuminating. I would also like to thank his wife, Mary, for initially getting in touch with me. I owe a special debt of gratitude to Simon Kennedy, the author of the fascinating fictionalised account of the boycott, *The Year the Whales Came In* (Dublin, 2004), who generously gave of his time, shared his research and painted a picture of some of the boycott's central characters. Nicky Furlong was also of

The Fethard-on-Sea Boycott

invaluable assistance in portraying the historical background to the boycott. My thanks go to Gerry Gregg and Eoghan Harris, who were involved in producing the film *A Love Divided*, for sharing their researches. I also wish to acknowledge the help given to me by Bernard Browne, John Carroll, Anne Cox, Richard Curry, Seamus de Vál, Maurice and Morgan Dockrell, Diarmaid Ferriter, the late Violet Grant, Conor Harnett, Anthony Hederman, Michael Laffan, Michael Lillis, Ted Nealon, Augusta and Michael Nicholson, Kevin B. Nowlan, Diarmaid Ó Muirithe, Cathal O'Shannon and Jonathan Williams, as well as the staff of the Central Catholic Library and its honorary librarian, Peter Costello; Joe Canning and the staff of the Ó Fiaich Memorial Library and Archive in Armagh; Noelle Dowling of the Dublin Diocesan Archives; Seamus Helferty and the staff of UCD Archives; Raymond Refaussé and the staff of the Church Representative Body Library; Grainne Doran of Wexford County Library HQ; and the staff of the National Archives of Ireland, the National Library of Ireland, Pearse Street Library and Wexford Town Public Library. Unfortunately, two requests – to Bishop Brendan Comiskey and Bishop Denis Brennan – for access to the Fethard-on-Sea Boycott file held by the Diocese of Ferns were refused. Though I consulted a wide variety of publications about Wexford's local history, Billy Colfer's painstakingly researched history of the region concerned, *The Hook Peninsula* (Cork, 2004), was of particular assistance to me when writing this book. Thanks to all at The Collins Press who were exceptionally helpful throughout the publication process. I am very grateful to Catalina Panadés Muret, in whose apartment in Palma de Mallorca much of this book was written. I also

Acknowledgements

want especially to thank Sandra, who constantly kept me going when I couldn't see the light at the end of the tunnel.

Finally, I must make special mention of my mother for her extraordinary patience and helpful remarks during endless conversations about 'Fethard', and my father who went to great lengths to help and encourage me.

Sources

Church of Ireland Representative Church Body Library
Typescript account by Rev. Edward Grant, former Church of Ireland Rector of the Fethard Union of Parishes, of the boycott, written from notes taken directly after meetings with the Catholic Bishop of Ferns, James Staunton, the Catholic Parish Priest of Templetown, Fr Laurence Allen, and the Catholic Curate in Charge of Poulfur, Fr William Stafford. The account also refers to incidents relevant to Catholic/Protestant relations before and after the boycott.

Dublin Diocesan Archives (DDA)
  McQuaid Papers.

National Archives of Ireland (NAI)
Attorney General's Office:
  AGO/2002/16/371.
Chief Secretary's Office:
  Registered Papers 1880-85.
Department of the Taoiseach:
  S16247 (Fethard-on-Sea Boycott 1957–58).

Sources

National Library of Ireland (NLI)
Sheehy Skeffington Papers:
> Owen Sheehy Skeffington correspondence re boycott MS 40515/8.

Ó Fiaich Memorial Library and Archive (OFMLA)
D'Alton Papers:
> Box 33, Custody of Children, Arch/12/15.

UCD Archives (UCDA)
Papers of Rev. Adrian Fisher – Fisher was the Rector of the Fethard Union of Parishes during the boycott. His papers include correspondence with a prospective replacement teacher for the Church of Ireland National School, Liam MacGabhann, and prominent Catholic and Protestant national figures, such as Eoin O'Mahony, A. A. Luce and E. H. Crosby-Lewis; notebooks; correspondence between Fisher and parishioners; minutes of the meetings of the Fethard Relief Fund; letters of support from Ireland – North and South – and abroad.

Private Collection
Seán Cloney's papers.

Newspapers and Periodicals
Belfast Newsletter
Belfast Telegraph
The Bell
Catholic Directory 1958–1964
Catholic Herald (London)
Church of Ireland Gazette
The Furrow
Irish Catholic
Irish Independent
Irish News
Irish Press, The
Irish Times, The
New Ross Standard

People (later Wexford People)
Pictorial/Irish Pictorial
Standard (later *Catholic Standard*)
Sunday Dispatch
Sunday Independent
Sunday Press, The
Waterford News (later amalgamated with the *Waterford Star*)
Waterford Star

Books, Articles and Essays

Adams, Michael, *Censorship: The Irish Experience* (Alabama, 1968).

Bolster, Evelyn, *The Knights of Saint Columbanus* (Dublin, 1979).

Bowman, John, *De Valera and the Ulster Question 1917–1973* (Oxford, 1982).

Browne, Noel, *Against the Tide* (Dublin, 1986).

Butler, Hubert, *Escape from the Anthill* (Mullingar, 1985).

Cloney, Seán, 'The Cloney Families of County Wexford' in Kevin Whelan (ed.), *Wexford: History and Society* (Dublin, 1987).

Colfer, Billy, *The Hook Peninsula* (Cork, 2004).

Connolly, Seán, *Religion and Society in Nineteenth-Century Ireland* (Dundalk, 1985).

Coogan, Tim Pat, *De Valera: Long Fellow, Long Shadow* (London, 1993)

Cooney, John, *John Charles McQuaid: Ruler of Catholic Ireland* (Dublin, 1999).

Doherty, Gabriel and Dermot Keogh (eds.), *De Valera's Irelands* (Cork, 2003).

Dunne, Tom, *Rebellions: Memoir, Memory and 1798* (Dublin, 2004).

Fanning, Ronan, *Independent Ireland* (Dublin, 1983).

Feeney, John, *John Charles McQuaid: The Man & the Mask* (Cork, 1974).

Ferriter, Diarmaid, *The Transformation of Ireland 1900–2000* (London, 2004).

Forde, Walter (ed.), *From Heritage to Hope: Christian Perspectives on the 1798 Bicentenary* (Gorey, 1998).

Foster, Roy, *Modern Ireland: 1600–1972* (London, 1982).

Sources

Gahan, Daniel J., 'New Ross, Scullabogue and the 1798 Rebellion in southwestern Wexford' in *The Past*, No. 21, 1998.

— *Rebellion! Ireland in 1798* (Dublin, 1998).

— 'The Scullabogue Massacre 1798' in *History Ireland* Vol. 4, No. 3, (Autumn, 1996).

Hart, Peter, *The I.R.A. & Its Enemies: Violence and Community in Cork 1916–1923* (Oxford, 1998).

Inglis, Tom, *Moral Monopoly: The Rise and Fall of the Catholic Church in Modern Ireland* (Dublin, 1998).

Kennedy, Simon, *The Year the Whales Came In* (Dublin, 2004).

Keogh, Dáire and Nicholas Furlong, *The Mighty Wave: The 1798 Rebellion in Wexford* (Dublin, 1996).

Keogh, Dermot, *Twentieth-Century Ireland: Nation and State* (Dublin, 1994)

— *Ireland and the Vatican: The Politics and Diplomacy of Church–State Relations 1922–1960* (Cork, 1995).

Lee, Joseph and Gearóid Ó Tuathaigh, *The Age of De Valera* (Dublin, 1982).

Lee, Joseph, *Ireland 1912–1985, Politics and Society* (Cambridge, 1989).

Longford, Earl of and T. P. O'Neill, *Éamon de Valera* (London, 1970).

Lyons, F. S. L., *Ireland since the Famine* (Glasgow, 1973).

MacDonagh, Oliver, *States of Mind: A Study of Anglo-Irish Conflict 1780–1980* (London, 1983).

Marlow, Joyce, *Captain Boycott & The Irish* (London, 1973).

Moloney, Ed, *Paisley: From Demagogue to Democrat?* (Dublin, 2008).

Murray, Patrick, *Oracles of God: The Roman Catholic Church and Irish Politics 1922–37* (Dublin, 2000).

O'Carroll, J. P. and John A. Murphy (eds.), *De Valera and His Times* (Cork, 1983).

O'Connor, Catherine, 'Mixed marriage, 'a grave injury to our church': An account of the 1957 Fethard-on-Sea Boycott' in *The History of the Family* Vol. 13 (2008).

The Fethard-on-Sea Boycott

Ó Corrain, Daithí, *Rendering to God and Caesar: The Irish Churches and the Two States in Ireland, 1949–73* (Manchester, 2006).

Pakenham, Thomas, *The Year of Liberty* (London, 1969).

Potterton, Homan, *Rathcormick: A Childhood Recalled* (London, 2004).

Rafter, Kevin, *The Clann: The Story of Clann na Poblachta* (Cork, 1996).

Ruddock, Norman, *The Rambling Rector* (Dublin, 2005).

Urwin, Margaret, *A County Wexford Family in the Land War: The O'Hanlon Walshs of Knocktartan* (Dublin, 2002).

Whelan, Kevin (ed.), *Wexford: History and Society* (Dublin, 1987).

— *The Tree of Liberty: Radicalism, Catholicism and the Construction of Irish Identity 1760–1830* (Cork, 1996).

White, Jack, *Minority Report: The Protestant Community in the Republic of Ireland* (Dublin, 1975).

Whyte, J. H., *Church and State in Modern Ireland 1923–1970* (Dublin, 1971).

Notes

Introduction

1 John McGahern, 'Reading and Writing' in Gabriel Doherty and Dermot Keogh (eds.), *De Valera's Irelands* (Cork, 2003), p. 132.
2 *The Irish Times*, 26 October 1999.

Chapter 2: Forgetting Scullabogue

1 Steven W. Myers and Delores E. McKnight (eds.), *Sir Richard Musgrave's Memoirs of the Irish Rebellion of 1798* (Fort Wayne, 1995), p. 400.
2 Colm Tóibín, 'New Ways of Killing Your Father' in *London Review of Books*, 18 November 1993.
3 Summary of the Ely Papers, Public Record Office of Northern Ireland.
4 Tom Dunne, *Rebellions: Memoir, Memory and 1798* (Dublin, 2004), p. 166.
5 Kevin Whelan, *The Tree of Liberty: Radicalism, Catholicism and the Construction of Irish Identity 1760–1830* (Cork, 1996), p. 10.
6 Daniel Gahan, 'The Scullabogue Massacre 1798' in *History Ireland*, (Autumn, 1996), p. 30.
7 Myers and McKnight (eds.), *Musgrave's Memoirs*, p. 351.

Chapter 3: Learning how to Boycott

1 *The Irish Times*, 7 September 1886.

The Fethard-on-Sea Boycott

2 *Ibid.*, 11 September 1886.

3 The curate was born Walsh but later added his mother's maiden name, perhaps in a bid to further Gaelicise his roots. To avoid confusion, I have referred to him throughout as O'Hanlon Walsh.

4 Quoted in Donald Jordan, 'The Irish National League and the unwritten law: rural protest and nation-building in Ireland, 1882–1890', *Past & Present*, (February 1998).

5 *People*, 11 August 1880.

6 *Ibid.*, 29 September 1880.

7 *Ibid.*, 11 October 1880.

8 Margaret Urwin, *A County Wexford Family in the Land War: The O'Hanlon Walshs of Knocktartan* (Dublin, 2002), p. 10.

9 The great survey of the productive capacity of land and rentable value of buildings undertaken by the Commissioner of Valuation, Richard Griffith, for the purpose of local taxation between 1848 and 1864.

10 Parnell was arrested on 13 October 1881, along with other leaders of the Land League, for using inflammatory language to attack Gladstone's second Land Act.

11 National Archives of Ireland, Chief Secretary's Office, Registered Papers 4222/85, RIC Report, 28 February 1883.

12 *Ibid.*, Robert Kennedy RM to Assistant Under Secretary, 4 March 1883.

13 The Land League gave way to the Irish National League by the end of 1882.

14 A three-pronged fork for dumping dung.

15 Myles Joyce was an elderly farmer convicted of the brutal murder of John Joyce and four members of his family in Maamtrasna, County Galway, on 17 August 1882, and subsequently hanged, despite his protestations of innocence; 'Red Jack' was Lord John Poyntz Spencer, the Lord Lieutenant, who was criticised by Nationalists for his handling of the case.

16 NAI CSO RP 4222/85, RIC report, 28 September 1884.

17 *Ibid.*, Kennedy to Under Secretary Hamilton, 12 November 1884.

18 *The Irish Times*, 16 December 1886.

19 *Ibid.*, 18 February 1887.

Notes

20 *Ibid.*, 19 February 1887.
21 *Ibid.*, 21 February 1887.

Chapter 4: Growing up in Fethard

1 Seán Cloney, 'The Cloney Families of County Wexford' in Kevin Whelan (ed.), *Wexford: History and Society* (Dublin, 1987), p. 340.
2 Unpublished memoir of Seán Cloney (hereafter cited as Cloney memoir), p. 2.
3 Cloney, 'The Cloney Families', p. 336.
4 *Ibid.*
5 Cloney memoir, p. 12.
6 *Ibid.*, p. 17.
7 *Ibid.*, p. 22.
8 First-hand typescript account of the beginning of the boycott by Rev. Edward F. Grant, Representative Church Body (RCB) Library, PC 52 – hereafter cited as Grant account.
9 Author's interview with Seán Cloney, 1999.

Chapter 5: Seán and Sheila

1 Reference to 'emigration' in handwritten note in Seán Cloney papers.
2 Handwritten note in Seán Cloney papers.
3 Hubert Butler, 'Boycott Village' in *Escape from the Anthill* (Mullingar, 1985), pp. 135-36.
4 Grant account.
5 *Ibid.*
6 Tilson v Tilson: *Irish Law Times Reports* (LXXXVI) 1952, pp. 49–73, quoted in J. H. Whyte, *Church and State in Modern Ireland 1923–1970* (Dublin, 1971), p. 168.
7 Whyte, *Church and State*, pp. 170–171.
8 Bunreacht na hÉireann 42.1.
9 Grant account.
10 *The Irish Times*, 10 May 1997.
11 Handwritten note in Seán Cloney's papers.
12 *The Irish Times*, 10 May 1997.
13 Author's interview with Eileen Cloney, 2007.

Chapter 6: News from the North

1 *Irish Independent*, 21 May 1957.
2 *People*, 11 May 1957.
3 Author's interview with Sheila Cloney, 3 January 2008.
4 *The Sunday Press*, 1 February 1987.
5 Notebook in Seán Cloney's papers.
6 *People*, 11 May 1957.

Chapter 7: The Boycott Begins

1 Grant account.
2 Author's interview with Adrian Fisher, 27 March 2007.
3 *Ibid.*
4 *Church of Ireland Gazette*, 17 May 1957.
5 Author's interview with David Gardiner, 17 May 2008.
6 *The Irish Times*, 27 May 1957.
7 *Sunday Independent*, 30 May 1957.
8 *Ibid.*, 6 June 1957.
9 Grant account.
10 It is worth noting that in the six months before Sheila Cloney's departure, when she was coming under sustained pressure to send her daughter Eileen to the Catholic school, there was no incumbent rector to proffer advice. The rector of the neighbouring Taghmon Union was providing pastoral care. It would be foolish to speculate upon what might have happened if Grant had still been rector during this period, but Sheila Cloney might at least have had someone she felt she could turn to outside her immediate family.
11 Grant account.
12 *Ibid.*
13 *Ibid.*
14 *Ibid.*
15 *Ibid.*
16 *Ibid.*
17 *Ibid.*
18 *Ibid.*

Notes

Chapter 8: War of Words

1 Author's interview with Cathal O'Shannon, 18 June 2007.

2 *The Irish Times*, 27 May 1957.

3 *Ibid.*

4 Cathal O'Shannon interview, 18 June 2007.

5 For an account of the Mother-and-Child controversy, see p. 118.

6 *The Irish Times*, 3 June 1957.

7 *Irish Independent*, 4 June 1957.

8 *The Irish Press*, 5 June 1957.

9 *The Irish Times*, 7 June 1957.

10 E. H. Lewis-Crosby to Adrian Fisher, 11 June 1957, Fisher Papers UCD Archives (UCDA).

11 Interview with Adrian Fisher, 27 March 2007.

12 *Irish Independent*, 6 June 1957.

13 *Belfast Telegraph*, 7 June 1957.

14 *The Irish Times*, 5 June 1957.

15 *Ibid.*, 29 May 1957.

16 J. H. Whyte, 'Political life in the South' in Michael Hurley (ed.), *Irish Anglicanism 1869–1969* (Dublin, 1970), p. 149.

17 W. B. Stanford, *A Recognized Church: the Church of Ireland in Eire* (Dublin, 1944), p. 17.

18 Seanad Debates, vol. 48, 5 June 1957.

19 *Ibid.* 109–10.

20 MacGabhann to Fisher, 11 June 1957, Fisher Papers, UCDA.

21 MacGabhann to D'Alton, 12 June 1957, *ibid.*

22 D'Alton to MacGabhann, 14 June 1957, *ibid.*

23 MacGabhann to Staunton, 18 June 1957, *ibid.*

24 Staunton to MacGabhann, 19 June 1957, *ibid.*

25 MacGabhann to Fisher, 1 July 1957, *ibid.*

26 Fisher to MacGabhann, 25 June 1957, *ibid.*

27 MacGabhann to Fisher, 1 July 1957, *ibid.*

28 *Belfast Telegraph*, 26 June 1957.

29 *Sunday Independent*, 30 June 1957.

30 Norman Ruddock, *The Rambling Rector* (Dublin, 2005), pp. 62–63.

31 *Ibid.*

32 Evelyn Bolster, *The Knights of Saint Columbanus* (Dublin, 1979).

33 *Standard*, 21 June 1957.

Chapter 9: Vigilantes and Gunmen

1 Author's interview with Simon Kennedy, 11 June 2007.

2 Author's interview with David Gardiner, 17 May 2008.

3 Seán Cloney interview, 1999.

4 Author's interview with David Gardiner, 17 May 2008.

5 Cloney memoir.

6 Author's interview with Ted Nealon, 2007.

7 Handwritten note in Seán Cloney papers.

Chapter 10: Knights and Bishops

1 Dermot Keogh, *Twentieth-Century Ireland: Nation and State* (Dublin, 1994), p. 209.

2 Bolster, *The Knights of Saint Columbanus*, pp. 18-19.

3 *Ibid.*, p. 20.

4 *Ibid.*, p. 51.

5 *Ibid.*, p. 53.

6 *Ibid.*, p. 90.

7 *Ibid.*, p. 33.

8 *Ibid.*, p. 43.

9 *Ibid.*, p. 93.

10 *Ibid.*, p. 239.

11 *The Irish Times*, 12 April 1957.

12 *Ibid.*, pp. 230–31.

13 Quoted in Whyte, *Church and State*, pp. 242–43.

14 Bolster, *op. cit.*, p. 107.

15 *Irish Catholic Directory 1963*, pp. 736–37.

16 Typescript of review written by Vincent Grogan of E. Bolster's *The Knights of St Columbanus*, contained in the files of the Attorney General's Office, NAI, AGO/2002/16/371.

17 Bolster, *The Knights of Saint Columbanus*, p. 108.

18 *Irish Independent*, 1 July 1957.

19 *People*, 6 July 1957.

20 *Free Press*, 5 July 1957.

21 Paul Blanshard, an American journalist and son of a Protestant clergyman, who specialised in anti-Catholic polemic, stirred things up further with the publication of *The Irish and Catholic Power* in 1954. Already the author of two books about the Catholic Church and its relationship with the civil state in the

Notes

United States, Blanshard, having spent over six months in Ireland in the early 1950s researching his book, had attacked the theocratic nature of the state. He reserved particular scorn for what he perceived as the obsequious deference shown by the government towards the leaders of the Church: 'In the case of the Irish government, the manners of the state's leader in dealing with Catholic dignitaries are definitely "colonial": the leaders of the Church are treated with that conspicuous deference which the subject peoples showed to British imperial dignitaries a century ago. An archbishop is treated with the adulation that might have been accorded to a medieval prince; and a cardinal is honoured like a king.' Blanshard was not optimistic about the future of the Protestant minority in the South, whom he said had 'no choice but to defend themselves against the most thoroughly regimented and most persistently aggressive religious oligarchy in the world'.

22 *Standard*, 5 July 1957.
23 *Ibid.*

Chapter 11: 'Against all our National Traditions'

1 Dermot Keogh, *Twentieth-Century Ireland* (1994), p. 229.
2 Dáil Debates, vol. 39.
3 J. H. Whyte, *Church & State*, p. 42.
4 Quoted in Keogh, *op. cit.*, p. 94.
5 Interview with Morgan Dockrell, 18 June 2007.
6 Author's interview with Ted Nealon, 2007.
7 Cabinet memo, NAI D/T S16247.
8 Draft letter from de Valera to Staunton, *ibid.*
9 Cabinet memo, *ibid.*
10 *Church of Ireland Gazette*, 14 June 1957.
11 Departmental memo, NAI D/T S16247.
12 John Cooney, *John Charles McQuaid: Ruler of Catholic Ireland* (Dublin, 1999), p. 321.
13 W. W. Magee to de Valera, NAI D/T S16247.
14 *The Irish Times*, 26 June 1957.
15 *Standard*, 5 July 1957.
16 A. A. Luce to de Valera, NAI D/T S16247.
17 *The Irish Times*, 3 July 1957.

18 NAI D/T S16247.
19 Dáil Debates, vol. 163, 4 July 1957.
20 Brendan Halligan (ed.), *The Brendan Corish Seminar Proceedings* (Dublin, 2006), p. 23.
21 Niamh Puirséil, *The Irish Labour Party 1922–73* (Dublin, 2007), p. 213.

Chapter 12: 'Not an Inch'

1 Luce to Fisher, 5 July 1957, Fisher Papers, UCDA.
2 Gore-Grimes to de Valera, 10 July 1957, NAI D/T S16247.
3 Ryan to de Valera, 9 July 1957, *ibid*.
4 *The Irish Press*, 6 July 1957.
5 *The Irish Times*, 9 May 1997.
6 *Ibid.*, 8 July 1957.
7 Letter from Seán Cloney to de Valera, D/T S16247, NAI.
8 Handwritten note in Seán Cloney's papers.
9 *The Irish Press*, 8 July 1957.

Chapter 13: 'Outside the Pale'

1 Census 2006: Vol. 13.
2 *The Irish Times*, 8 June 1957.
3 Morgan Dockrell's father, Maurice, was a Fine Gael TD in Dublin for thirty-four years and Lord Mayor 1960/61. As one of the Protestant members of the Dáil, he met with the Taoiseach, Éamon de Valera, to discuss the boycott and had found him sympathetic – author's interview with Morgan Dockrell, 18 June 2007.
4 *Ibid.*
5 *Church of Ireland Gazette*, 21 June 1957.
6 *The Irish Times*, 8 June 1957.
7 Butler to Owen Sheehy Skeffington, 20 June 1957, Sheehy Skeffington Papers MS 40515/8.
8 Butler, *Escape from the Anthill*, p. 138.
9 *The Irish Times*, 12 June 1957.
10 *Ibid.*, 13 June 1957.
11 Grant account.
12 *Ibid.*

Notes

13 *Church of Ireland Gazette*, 5 July 1957.

14 *The Irish Press*, 21 June 1957.

15 *Belfast Newsletter*, 11 July 1957.

16 D'Alton to Staunton, 9 July, 1959, D'Alton Papers Arch/12/15
   Ó Fiaich Memorial Library and Archive.

17 Staunton to D'Alton, 10 July 1959, *ibid.*

18 *The Irish Press*, 13 July 1957.

19 *The Irish Times*, 13 July 1957.

20 *Ibid.*, 15 July 1957.

21 *Standard*, 19 July 1957.

22 *Ibid.*, 26 July 1957.

23 Fisher Papers.

24 *Belfast Telegraph*, 27 August 1957.

25 Fisher Papers.

Chapter 14: The Secret Deal

1 *The Irish Press*, 9 July 1957.

2 NAI D/T S16247.

3 Author's interview with Anthony Hederman, 30 November 2009.

4 *The Irish Press*, 7 August 1957.

5 Auld to Sullivan, 13 August 1957.

6 *The Irish Times*, 8 August 1957.

7 *Ibid.*, 8 August 1957.

8 *Ibid.*, 10 August 1957.

9 *Belfast Telegraph*, 24 September 1957.

10 *Church of Ireland Gazette*, 25 October 1957.

11 *People*, 12 January 1958.

12 *Sunday Dispatch*, 7 January 1958.

Chapter 15: The Aftermath

1 Staunton to McQuaid, 21 January 1958, McQuaid Papers,
   Dublin Diocesan Archives (DDA).

2 *The Irish Times*, 5 March 1973.

3 Butler, *Escape from the Anthill*, p. 141.

4 *The Irish Times*, 9 May 1997.

5 *Sunday Tribune*, 16 May 1999.

6 *The Irish Times*, 10 May 1997.

7 *Sunday Press*, 1 February 1987.
8 *The Irish Times*, 1 June 1998.
9 *Ibid.*, 6 June 1998.

Appendix: The Catholic Public Relations Bureau

1 Report of the advisory committee to the hierarchy, 17 June 1957, McQuaid Papers, DDA.
2 *Ibid.*
3 *Ibid.*
4 Preliminary report of the Committee on Documentation and Public Opinion, 8 January 1958, McQuaid Papers, DDA.
5 *Ibid.*
6 Staunton to McQuaid, 15 January 1958, McQuaid Papers, DDA.
7 Fergus to Patrick Kilroy, 18 January 1958, McQuaid Papers, DDA.
8 Fr James Kavanagh to McQuaid, 7 February 1958, McQuaid Papers, DDA.
9 McQuaid memo of meeting with Committee on Documentation and Public Opinion, 7 February 1958, McQuaid Papers, DDA.

Index

Index

Index